Outrage 2000

Levie Kanes

gefen
publishing house בית הוצאה לאור
JERUSALEM ◆ NEW YORK

Typesetting: Raphaël Freeman, Jerusalem Typesetting
Cover Design: S. Kim Glassman

ISBN 965-229-319-9

1   3   5   7   9   8   6   4   2

Gefen Publishing House
6 Hatzvi Street, Jerusalem 91360, Israel
972-2-538-0247 • orders@gefenpublishing.com

Gefen Books
12 New Street, Hewlett, NY 11557, USA
516-295-2805 • orders@gefenpublishing.com

www.israelbooks.com

Printed in Israel

Send for our free catalogue

Acknowledgments

I DEDICATE THIS BOOK to my dear wife, Dr. Ofelia Kanes, who has always been a source of support and inspiration. Special thanks to Dr. Frans Govers for sharing information and to Nancy Siciliana for helping me edit my first manuscript and to my son Soly for sharing his army experiences. I dedicate this book to the memory of my late mother, Caroline Nathan Kanes (Kallus), David Kallus and my sister, Henriette Kallus.

I want to acknowledge the dedication and effort of Mrs. Sorelle Weinstein in the final editing of my manuscript. Her insight and foresight helped me express my thoughts with increased clarity. It is my hope that *Outrage* will become a volume that is required reading in high schools; perhaps in this way, future generations will have the vision to prevent another Holocaust upon the Jews, who were a defenseless, benign population then, and a people still struggling to survive.

Author's Note

OUTRAGE IS THE STORY of my rescue, after I had been stolen from my mother during the Holocaust. The title of this book seemed appropriate in light of my outrage at the brutality imposed upon the Jewish people, and more specifically, upon my family. As a people, we did not pose a threat to anyone, yet the world permitted unspeakable atrocities to be committed against us.

My childhood was filled with the sound of my mother's heartbreaking sobs in our home in Montreal. Her descriptions of the events that shaped her young adulthood, and marred her old age, are embedded in my memories as a boy and as a man. Indeed, my mother's narrative of the events related in this book were so vivid in my childhood and adult imagination, it was as if each of the characters had been given a voice, and were speaking directly to the reader.

A collection of photographs is also included in this work to provide an invaluable record of corroboration for the incidents detailed in my book. Although I tried to be as accurate as possible with regards to the names of the characters, I occasionally had to use a pseudonym so as to protect the privacy of certain individuals. Another reason for the use of pseudonyms is that the true identities of several people remained hidden from either my mother (who died in 1985) or from myself. These pseudonyms are duly indicated in the text.

Contents

Introduction

AT APPROXIMATELY 11:00 P.M. on December 31, 1999, El Al flight 338 began its final voyage for the year from Amsterdam to Tel Aviv. It left on schedule. The Schiphol airport in Amsterdam was already coming to a standstill, as Dutch travellers awaited the potential tumult of the Y2K bug on January 1, 2000. Air traffic that night was sparse. The plane broke through the clouds and the sun illuminated the cabin, as I made myself comfortable in my seat. I revelled in the fact that I was assigned to a row that was spacious and gloriously empty. Being six feet, six inches tall with unusually long legs normally means that I have to force my legs into a cramped, confined space. Inadequate legroom has been my reality for as long as I can remember. I was grateful for the extra space and for the fact that less than fifty other passengers had boarded the plane with me.

My purpose in travelling to Holland that December was to uncover information about my family's history – to learn about, and verify, the fate of many of the family members from whom I had been separated as a result of the war. During my trip, I had obtained a thirty-five-page report on my family's history there, written by a relative on my father's side. I had no idea what would be revealed in its pages, and I took advantage of the relative peace and solitude on the flight to reflect upon my family. I belonged to a family that once exceeded five hundred members. With the exception of myself, and four other surviving family members, all five hundred perished in the Nazi occupation of Holland during World War Two. Fifty-five years later, as the world prepared to enter a new millennium, I was still living with the effects of the Holocaust upon myself and my family.

Despite my eagerness to glean as much information as possible about my family, I could not possibly have been prepared for the gruesome accounts that awaited me. As I turned the pages of the report, the horrors of the Holocaust unfolded. I read about how my grandfather (and namesake), Levie Kanes, and his wife, Esther Hamburg, perished at the Sobibor death camp on April 23, 1943. About how their eldest son, Maurits Kanes, together with his wife, Rebecca Winnik, and their two small children, were exterminated at Auschwitz on July 29, 1942. And about their daughter, Anna Kanes, and her husband, Ezechiel Bruinvelds, who were also killed at Sobibor. My father, Salomon Kanes, was murdered on January 16, 1944 in Auschwitz. While I had been aware of the fates of some of my immediate family members, this report detailed the murder of hundreds of cousins I had never even known existed.

My story begins with my separation from my mother shortly after I was born: she silently complied as a Dutch nurse smuggled me off the train that was headed for the labor camp, Westerbork. It was only after my mother had survived the hell of Auschwitz, and the likes of Josef Mengele, that she was able to set out to find me.

As I read through the report, which graphically described the brutal experiences of my family, I was engulfed by a torrent of sadness and pain. The information was too much to take in at once; I had to stop reading. I put the report down slowly, and attempted to breathe, as I suddenly felt a lack of oxygen. I experienced deep anguish, and feared that I was suffering from a heart attack. Tears poured down my cheeks, and I slumped over in my seat. I wanted to allow myself to absorb these strong emotions of anger and sadness at what I had just read.

I could not comprehend the destruction of so many children, nor could I imagine what the adults had been thinking as they were forced onto the trains like livestock. If not for the fact that I knew, from first-hand experience and from the experiences of family members, that these atrocities actually did happen, I would never have believed such horrors possible. Because of the Nazi cruelty against the Jews, I was deprived of knowing, and in turn loving, most of my family.

I reflected on the fact that never since the dawn of history had the world witnessed such a campaign of extermination. The war was not ignited by religious fanatics or instigators of pogroms – the government had been taken over by murderers, who were given the authority to hunt down and kill anyone they deemed to be a threat to their plans: men and women, old and young, healthy and sick; Jews, gypsies, and anyone else opposed to their regime.

The method of extermination was twofold: the victims were to be tortured, degraded, and humiliated, so that they were stripped of their last shreds of dignity and strength. Then, the state agencies would bring the victims from all over Hitler's Europe to the death camps, where they were mercilessly murdered. They were either killed individually, or en masse by the murderers' bullets, standing over graves dug by the victims themselves, or in slaughterhouses constructed especially for human beings.

For the condemned, there was no judge to whom to appeal for a redress of injustice; no government from which to ask protection and punishment for the murderers; no neighbor on whose door to knock. Without doubt, the Nazis would not have been so successful in exterminating so many hundreds of thousands of Dutch Jews without the collaboration of the state institutions, and the Dutch police in particular.

I still find it difficult to accept that German society of that time, which was supposed to comprise the most educated and sophisticated people in the world, would allow, and actively facilitate, the commission of the atrocities of the Holocaust. It is even more unfathomable that in the aftermath of the Holocaust, there are revisionists like David Irving, an alleged "historian" who denies that the Holocaust ever took place. It seems incomprehensible that a libel action he brought against Deborah Lipstadt, a professor of Modern Jewish and Holocaust Studies at Emory University in Atlanta, would ever be taken seriously. But, absurdly, his legal action forced Lipstadt to prove in a court of law that the Holocaust and gas chambers had actually existed. The trial had been receiving a great deal of attention at the time of my trip, and I could not fail to recognize its relevance to my own story.

I had always wished that there was something I could have done during the war, something that would have made a difference, but now my outrage at Irving's lawsuit forced me into a decision. I knew, at that moment on the nearly empty plane, that I would write this book so that everyone would know our story. I also wanted to ensure that the bravery displayed by many heroic Dutch people, Catholics and Protestants, would be publicized. Their courage saved many Jews from death. The extraordinary story of their unselfish efforts, and the experiences of the few survivors of the Holocaust, is a history that must be told. Education is our only defense against future attempts by Holocaust deniers, such as Irving, to distort and rewrite history. It is the best insurance against further insult toward the victims of the Holocaust and their families.

Prologue

DR. JACOB COHEN enjoyed his coffee in the cafeteria of the Haagse General Hospital, savoring the stillness of the room around him, as well as the rich flavor of his drink. His morning had been extraordinarily hectic. After delivering several babies, as well as performing an emergency appendectomy, he was in desperate need of a rest. As he sipped his coffee, he considered his position and work at the hospital.

The coffee was a decadent, rare treat; it was virtually impossible to obtain it, even on the black market. But since the Haagse General Hospital had been transferred to German management, the absence of such "luxuries" was not felt. The doctors and senior staff received abundant supplies of food and drink, while everyone else was forced to do without. Dr. Cohen considered his daily caffeine intake one of the few rewards of working in such a place. Still deep in thought, he noticed Dr. Shultz (pseudonym), formerly of the Berlin Medical Institution, standing in the corner of the cafeteria, glaring in his direction.

Cohen dutifully nodded at Shultz, and promptly remembered his responsibilities in the wards. Shultz was not simply a doctor who now managed the hospital, he was also a high-ranking SS officer and a personal

friend of *Reichkomissionar* Arthur Seyss-Inquart, whose friendship with
Hitler was well known.

In his capacity as an officer of the SS, Shultz was in charge of the civil
administration in the Netherlands. Cohen reflected upon how much Shultz
despised him, and indeed all Jews. He did not need to be reminded that
he had only been spared the bitter wrath that fell upon all Jews because
his skills as a doctor were desperately needed at the hospital. As much
as possible, Cohen avoided coming into contact with Shultz, and other
doctors like him, while maintaining an appearance of cooperation. Shultz
suspected that Cohen was using his position in the hospital to clandestinely
help other Jews.

The doctor was shaken out of his thoughts when the nurse pulled at
his arm. She spoke abruptly, asking him to please hurry to the maternity
ward, as the tall woman from The Hague had gone into labor. He gulped
down the rest of his coffee, and followed the nurse up to the maternity
ward. One glance at his patient, Caroline Kanes (née Nathan), told him
that she was ready to deliver. The midwife was coaching Caroline to take
deep breaths; the baby's head was already crowning.

Dr. Cohen immediately went to work, almost as if he had been pro-
grammed into action. He pulled on his sterilized gloves and completed
the delivery within a few minutes. Once the nurse had cleaned the baby,
and wrapped him up warmly, the doctor handed the newborn over to his
fatigued but elated mother. Cohen found himself strangely attracted to
this new mother, as he watched her hold and caress her infant son. Her
breasts were beautiful and full, with tantalizing, pink, erect nipples. Her
body, even after the trauma of pregnancy and labor, was firm and slender.
He suddenly felt as if he was the only other person in the ward with her,
as his gaze locked on this beautiful woman. He was blissfully unaware of
those around him.

Caroline held her precious baby close to her chest, and motioned
to one of the nurses to bring her some material to cover herself. She felt
distinctly uncomfortable being exposed in this way, especially since she
felt the doctor's eyes bore into her.

Cohen was finally woken from his reverie by the clock; it was nearly
three o' clock, and he painfully recalled that he was supposed to be in Dr.
Shultz's office for their daily meeting. Shultz wanted to find out from Cohen
which of his patients were healthy enough to be sent to Westerbork, the

Dutch transit-labor camp. Every day, the two doctors would review the medical dossiers of each of Cohen's patients, and would determine who was sufficiently healthy for travel and work. Those who had received a clean bill of health were immediately sent off to the camp. More than once, Cohen had felt nauseating pangs of guilt at the thought that he was an accomplice to sending these poor unsuspecting patients to the labor camps. He knew that his signature on a patient file was tantamount to a death sentence; it effectively was responsible for sending those patients, Jews just as he, to a destination from which no one had ever returned.

To compound Cohen's discomfort, Shultz made his contempt for Cohen painfully obvious. Over time, however, Cohen learned to silence his conscience by reminding himself that at least he and his family were kept safe as a result of his position at the hospital.

Dr. Shultz was already seated at his desk, reviewing a stack of dossiers, when Cohen knocked on his door. "Come in," Schultz called out, without looking up from his papers.

Shultz had to admit that he admired Cohen's skill as a doctor, but the fact remained that he was a Jew, and so he loathed him. He only tolerated Cohen's "collaboration" at the hospital because Nazi policy forbade Germans to "soil their hands" in the medical treatment of Jews. Only Jewish doctors could treat Jewish patients, and medical treatment was necessary in preparing the Jewish patients for the work camps.

Since Cohen was a Jew himself, his presence at the hospital, among the patients, was reassuring. The Jewish patients were soothed by their doctor's assurances that they would only be sent to labor camps, where they could work until the end of the war. It was essential that the patients were not aware of their true fate, because they were less likely to cause trouble, and resist their transportation, if they felt that their lives were not endangered.

To Shultz, Cohen was as detestable as he was necessary. He eagerly awaited the day when he could send the smug Cohen to his death. Shultz knew from his friend Seyss-Inquart that Holland was the only country in Europe that the Nazis wished to incorporate into a greater Germany. The Dutch were a perfect example of "superior racial quality," certifiably 100 percent Aryan. The problem with Holland, however, was that of the nine million people living in the country, some 140,000 were Jews. The Nazis obsessed about "the Jewish Problem" all over Europe, but nowhere would this obsession be nursed more ferociously than in Holland. Dutch genes were indeed a handsome booty, but it would be necessary to rid Holland of its Jews altogether if it was to become part of the greater German nation.

Shultz knew that if this incorporation were to successfully take place, he would have to help speed the process of eliminating Jews. Furthermore, Shultz had just received word that the Nazis had been forced to surrender at Stalingrad. This was the first time the German Army had suffered such a loss. As a result, Nazi restrictions were expected to tighten, and the need for laborers to intensify, as the Nazis increased their armament production. One way of facilitating this renewed war effort was to send healthy women to work in the factories as soon as they were able to leave the hospital. Shultz intended to achieve this goal as quickly as possible with Cohen's help.

Schultz wasted no time in demanding Cohen's signature on the dossiers of the latest batch of patients so that they could be dispatched to the Westerbork transit camp as early as that evening. "Are Mevrouw, Cohen, Fishbein, and Elsas ready to leave with their babies?" he asked, placing the stack of files in front of Cohen so that he could sign them. Aware that he could no longer manufacture excuses for these women, he reluctantly confirmed his patients' health.

"They are all ready to go," Cohen replied.

As he signed each release order, more dossiers were shoved under his nose for his signature.

*

In Ward Six of the hospital, the nurses brought the newborn babies to their mothers for a feeding. Caroline Kanes held her baby son lovingly, as she examined and admired his fine features and his full head of black hair. His perfect hands with their delicate, long fingers were just like those of her husband, Soli. The baby had weighed nearly ten pounds at birth, and was a healthy twenty inches long. He is going to be a real heavyweight, Caroline thought, unlike his father, who only fell into the middleweight category. Caroline could only hope that her husband was safe in his internment at Westerbork. She had not heard news from Soli in a long time. Betsy Elsas, a woman who had also just given birth, nursed her young infant alongside Caroline. She, too, had been separated from her husband for a number of months, and was ignorant of his fate in the Westerbork camp.

When Dr. Cohen walked into the ward to check on his patients, he approached Betsy first. He had come to tell her that she was ready to be discharged, but took advantage of his close proximity to Caroline to stare at her once more. Cohen attempted to reassure and encourage Betsy with his words. She was seemingly anxious about her safety, and that of her baby, in the upcoming trip.

"I performed the circumcision a few days ago," he said. "You and your baby boy are free to travel now. You will soon be reunited with your husband, and everything will be all right." Betsy had every reason to be nervous about their future, and Dr. Cohen mustered all of his strength to maintain the facade. Betsy feigned happiness at the thought of being reunited with her husband at the camp.

As Caroline watched Cohen glance at her surreptitiously, she was filled with disgust. She hated the way he looked at her and was disgusted at his lewd attempts to touch her during what was supposed to be a routine medical examination. Caroline did not believe Cohen's reassurances about the camp and suspected that he was deceiving Betsy. She was impatient for him to leave the ward, and remained silent once Betsy and the doctor had finished talking.

Caroline was relieved to see the doctor finally exit the ward, and wasted no time in leaning over to talk to Betsy. "Tell Soli he has a son," she said, talking in muted tones, so as not to disturb the baby as he nursed. "Tell him the boy's name is Levie, in memory of his grandfather. Oh, and please tell him I'll be coming to join him in a few days myself."

Betsy nodded, smiling in response, as she stroked her baby's body softly.

Caroline started to think of her other family members. Her in-laws had been sent to the camp three months earlier, and since then, she had heard no news from them either. As she sunk deeper and deeper into thought about her loved ones, and their safety, she noticed that Baby Levie had become sleepy, so she burped him and prepared to go to sleep herself. She was exhausted from giving birth, and knew it would not be long before she would be sent off to join her husband in Westerbork. Her thoughts were filled with memories….

ONE LAST SEDER

Chapter 1
German Invasion

Rotterdam, May 1940

ON FRIDAY MORNING, May 10, 1940, at six A.M., Caroline Nathan was beginning to stir in her sleep, and turned over to the other side in her bed. Her sister Elizabeth rushed into her room, and shook her excitedly, "Caroline, Caroline, wake up, look at the hundreds of airplanes in the sky!"

Caroline woke up to the droning of airplanes overhead. The rest of her family was already assembled in the living room, as they listened to the radio announcement that informed them that the Germans had invaded Holland and declared war.

Caroline's brothers, Isaac (Ies, to his family and friends) and Bram, had gone outside to look at the planes flying low above the city, and called out to the rest of the family to come and observe the spectacle. They looked up to the sky and saw hundreds of parachutists floating down on and around Rotterdam, positioning themselves in strategic locations.

That day, German forces destroyed most of the Dutch military planes and took control of the airfields around Rotterdam and The Hague. There was fierce resistance against an elite unit of German parachutists that attempted capturing Queen Wilhelmina and her family, but this particular force was largely eliminated. Elsewhere, the Germans were gaining ground, penetrating Fortress Holland with airborne troops. Although land-based German armies found pockets of strong resistance in the areas along the Big Rivers, much of southern Holland succumbed easily.

The situation deteriorated so quickly that just two days later, Queen Wilhelmina was informed by chief of staff, General Winkelman, that her safety could no longer be ensured. The Queen, her daughter Crown Princess Juliana, and her husband, Prince Bernard, left for England, accompanied by the senior ministers of the Dutch government. In England, Queen Wilhelmina released a statement explaining the reasons for her decision to leave the country: to protect the interests of Holland, to retain her freedom of action (which she could not have done in captivity), and to safeguard the interests of the Dutch East Indies. Queen Wilhelmina declared that she would fight the Germans to the best of her ability until they were driven from the country. She declared London to now be the capital of Holland, which assured the country's legal assistance and ability to continue in the war as one of the Allies.

By Tuesday, May 14, the situation was hopeless. Fortress Holland had virtually collapsed, but the Germans were impatient. What they had envisioned as a one-day operation was now in its fifth day. The Germans made it known that if the Dutch didn't surrender immediately, they would begin to systematically level Dutch cities. General Winkelman began negotiating the surrender as a means of avoiding bombardment of residential areas.

Caroline went shopping on the Jonker Frans Straat that day, accompanied by Elizabeth and Bram. At about 1:30 P.M., German planes appeared over the skies of the city. At first, the trio thought that these were more Heinkels to reinforce the German presence in Holland, when suddenly they heard the sound of the bombs whistling downward. During the long whistling sound, the siblings could see the explosions several miles away and feel the earth tremble. The whistling noise then became shorter and shorter as the bombs landed closer to them. Buildings exploded everywhere; flames raged throughout the woods. People were screaming and panicking as Rotterdam started to collapse around them.

Bram, Caroline, and Elizabeth found refuge in a basement of a German-occupied building, one of the few structures that had not suffered a hit. Nevertheless, they were terrified. The magnitude of the noise and the trembling of the ground was enough to drive anyone insane.

The accuracy of the German bombs was amazing. They had pinpointed their targets to perfection, leaving all railroads and buildings they had occupied intact. As suddenly as the bombing had started, so did it end. The Nazis had bombed Rotterdam only once, but in great force, starting from the center of the city and then spreading outwards.

Caroline and her siblings were eager to return home to ensure the safety of the rest of their family. They emerged from the basement to find destruction and chaos. They could hardly breathe – the smoke and dust were so unbearable. Almost all of the stores around them were on fire. Looters exploited the situation to steal whatever they could, since the owners could not prevent the theft of whatever could be salvaged. Bodies and limbs were scattered in the street, and the wailing ambulances could not pass through most places in the shattered city.

The three passed the pride of Rotterdam, the once beautiful cathedral of Saint Laurens Kerk, which was now severely damaged. They were relieved to find their home still intact with only shattered windows. Luckily, the rest of the family was safe.

Holland officially surrendered the next day, paying a heavy price. About forty thousand people had lost their lives and Rotterdam was in ruins. The country was now conquered; the unthinkable had already happened.

Several months after the surrender, on a mild October winter evening, Ies, Caroline, and Aaron Nathan opened the front door of their small but cosy apartment on Telmaa Straat in Rotterdam and welcomed their friends, Moshe Hamburg, Soli Kanes, and Jaap Praag. The group filed into the Nathans' warm, bright living room. Ies was twenty-six years old and active in the Jewish Defense League. He had helped establish the group with the aim of protecting vulnerable Jews in their communities from the growing Nazi threat. He and his friends believed that their work was desperately necessary, since in Austria and Germany, Nazi sympathizers had attacked many Jewish communities. The violence inflicted by the Nazi sympathizers was a common feature of daily life during these times.

In Holland, the NSB (the Dutch Nazi Party), led by Anton Mussert, had already succeeded in declaring themselves the only legal political party in the country. The organized raids in the Jewish districts of Amsterdam had begun to occur with increasing frequency. Life in Holland, as they once knew it, was changing irrevocably for the worst, just as it had already begun to do throughout other European countries controlled by Nazi forces.

Ies and his friends and family were not meeting for social reasons, although they shared a common bond of love and affection; they had a very specific goal in mind – to discuss politics and possible solutions to these new dangers. Ies loved Holland. He had been born there and had grown up in the Dutch Jewish tradition, with friends from every cultural and racial background. Holland had a unique history of tolerance and protection. As early as 1492, the time of the Spanish Inquisition, persecuted Jews had found refuge in Holland, safe from the brutality that was rampant in other parts of Europe. When France persecuted the Huguenots in the seventeenth century, Holland had provided a safe asylum. Many people of color from all over the world were able to live in Holland without fear of the discrimination and violence of slavery that could have been imposed on them elsewhere. After 1800, during Napoleon's occupation, Jews in Holland became full members of the trade guilds, and were allowed to participate freely in national politics. Freedom of religion had become a protected right in Holland.

Pogroms, an ugly reality in other countries, were unknown to Dutch Jews, and as a result, Amsterdam flourished as one of Europe's greatest centers of Jewish scholarship. Dutch history aside, there now seemed to be enough anti-Semitism in any given community to alert Jews to the potential dangers. Jews were conspicuous in their dress and customs, and were therefore a vulnerable target for Jew-baiters. Jews were hated and resented because of the promise contained in the Bible that the Jews would be granted their own homeland. Many suspected this Divine promise forged a strong bond of fraternity amongst the Jews that would override any fidelity to their nationality. Anti-Semites reasoned that Jews could never be trusted in matters of patriotic integrity, as they were loyal only to their own people.

A lifelong Zionist, Ies dreamed of the day that the Jews would have their own homeland, with an army to defend themselves. History had provided no shortage of examples of hatred directed toward the Jews in every country, in every era. He had come to the realization that Jews could only be safe in their own country, where they could build a future free of suffering and hatred.

"Please, everyone, make yourselves comfortable and sit down," Ies said graciously, as he surveyed the faces of his siblings and old friends. Caroline smiled graciously as she poured each of the guests a small, steaming cup of coffee and passed around a tray of fragrant buttercake. She was radiant in a lovely green silk dress, which she had carefully selected in honor of their guests. This was the first time she was meeting her brothers' friends, and she wanted to feel pretty, and charming in the company of these young men.

Everyone talked animatedly while Aaron drew the living room drapes together so that they could not be observed by passersby.

"Would you like some sugar in your coffee?" Caroline asked as she approached the handsome young man she knew as Soli.

Soli raised his eyes to her, and was unable to find the words to respond. He silently lifted his cup and saucer toward Caroline, and allowed her to drop a teaspoon of sugar in his cup.

Soli felt as if he were a schoolboy once more, with a crush on the most beautiful girl in his class: he smiled broadly, but had temporarily lost the power of speech. "Thank you," he said shyly, when he finally mustered the courage to speak. His eyes were locked on Caroline. He smiled, timidly at first, then more confidently, when he could see that his feelings for her were reciprocated.

Caroline returned Soli's interest with her own delighted smile. "Clientje," said Ies teasingly, using his pet name for his sister, "don't forget our other guests." It was as clear as day that his sister and best friend were smitten with each other. The couple quickly looked away from each other, as they realized that they were not alone, and were being watched by their friends. Their faces turned a deep shade of scarlet, and Caroline abruptly turned away to offer someone else – anyone else! – cream or sugar in his coffee.

Soli marvelled at the beautiful sight of Caroline, as she graciously moved around the room. He felt blood rushing to his veins, and could only look down at his knees as his face became increasingly red.

The group chatted and exchanged pleasantries, and Caroline was anxious for the serious discussions to begin. She had come to expect nothing less from Ies. She would occasionally look up from her coffee to find Soli still smiling in her direction, as the voices rose around her. His attention filled her with a glorious warmth inside, especially when Soli would beam silently at her while the others argued. Soli and Ies had been friends since childhood. Soli and Ies shared the same age and a love of boxing. They had met in the Macabee Sports Club where they fought against each other in the Dutch Golden Gloves competition in 1932. Soli had beaten Ies by three rounds, and had gone on to win the Golden Glove tournament.

Of all the many occasions that Soli had seen Caroline over the years, this was the first time that he viewed her as a lovely, young woman, and not as his best friend's younger sister. Ies had secretly hoped, when he organized this meeting, that his sister would be interested in Soli. Ies had plans for his future, which did not necessarily involve staying put. He wanted to be sure Caroline would always be cared for, even if he could not physically be there to look after her. Soli possessed many fine qualities: he was tall and handsome, an excellent boxer, and someone for whom he had a great deal of love and respect. Ies was excited to see that sparks indeed flew between his best friend and sister. Caroline was doing her best to concentrate on the discussion, while looking after the other guests, but her mind was really only on one person.

The first topic of discussion was the exit of the Netherlands royal family, along with some 4,500 Dutch officers, soldiers, and policemen. They had staged a Dutch Dunkirk, assisted by remnants of the country's Navy and the entire merchant marine. The swift German victory, combined with Queen Wilhemina's abandonment of the Dutch population, had disillusioned and embittered many Dutchmen. In Dutch circles, Ies was considered to be the most knowledgeable because he had just as many gentile friends as he did Jewish ones. He was considered the most qualified to expound on this situation.

"The evacuation to Britain of the royal family, along with a cadre of the Dutch government, has to be seen as critical in establishing a government in exile and the initial intelligence network in Holland…. An acquaintance of mine, the well-known Rotterdam lawyer, Dr. Johan Stijkel, has told me, in confidence, that he is organizing a resistance group of young Dutch citizens at the insistence of her Majesty. He will be aided by Major General H.D.S. Husselman and Colonel J.P. Bolton. They will keep the exile government informed of the events and wait for instructions. The Queen will continue to direct the Dutch resistance and finance all operations in Holland."

The group reassured Ies that they would cooperate as much as possible with this new group in formation, and everyone expressed relief when they were informed of the Queen's motives. The topic then switched to the many changes that had been occurring in their city since the Nazis had risen to power. News from other cities in Europe about Jews and their experiences under Nazi power was now a growing cause for concern in many circles. After listening to the conversation of her brothers and his friends, Caroline could see that the men were readying themselves for the action that was inevitable. They would have to be prepared to defend themselves, if necessary.

Soli suddenly turned to Caroline, and asked for her opinion on the subject. "Caroline, what do you think? How do you assess the situation? Some womanly intuition would not be amiss in this discussion."

Caroline thought for a minute before she faced all four men with her answer.

"Compared to cities like Warsaw and other occupied cities in Europe, the Germans are behaving decently in Holland. We don't see any looting or burning of synagogues here. Even the Germans who visit the French Bazaar seem polite. They are good customers."

"But," interrupted Ies with his analysis of the situation, "I think the Nazis want to entice the Dutch into embracing their 'New Order.' That's why they seem to be taking such pains in their 'shows' of good faith. 'Shows' are just what they are. They liberate the army and allow the men to return home to their families, but now we know all that is changing drastically."

"Yes, this is true," said Aaron. "First, Seyss-Inquart declares that the Nazis 'would not impose their ideology on Holland.' Do you remember how they were supposed to respect the existing Dutch laws? Well, we all thought that would work. Dutch laws are good laws, because they respect us as a people. Now we all know what a lie that has been.

"They invade in May, and sure enough, by July, they have already passed the first anti-Jewish edict. At first, Jews were forbidden to serve as volunteer air raid wardens, which is not really such a big deal in itself, but then they ban our ritual slaughtering!"

"They act like this is a law to protect the animals! These edicts have taken their toll on our community," said Jaap. "Just a couple of months ago, they passed laws forbidding us to work in the civil service, and then to stay out of the markets. The last straw is forcing Jewish businesses to register themselves so that they are identifiable to the Germans. There's no doubt about it that they are stepping up their persecutions. The real question is, where will it end?"

Certainly, there was a striking resemblance between the German Nazis and the Nazis who had occupied Holland. It was clear that soon all of the Dutch laws would be repealed or replaced by new dictates, which were intended to be extremely cruel towards the Jews. Ies and his friends felt the time had come for them to be prepared to defend themselves against this looming danger.

Ies organized groups of young men to keep watch over the community and prepare for the worst. He and Moshe both were members of Habonim, a Zionist movement that held cultural meetings and sports competitions. Habonim had about six hundred members who shared many of the concerns expressed by Ies and the other young men in the room. Moshe proposed that they form action groups to prepare themselves for roles in self-defense and defending their community. Everyone present agreed to take part. They divided the duties among themselves: Ies would be in charge of organizing the action groups for Rotterdam, while Aaron would do the same for The Hague. Soli, Moshe, and Jaap would be in charge of organizing the main point in Amsterdam. They concluded their discussion by agreeing to meet the following week in Amsterdam, where they would discuss further their plans of action.

After wrapping up their discussion, Soli moved to sit next to Caroline, and tried to start conversation with her. She was a real beauty, and Soli knew that he had to be on his best behavior with Ies as his best friend. He certainly didn't want to say anything that would make her think he was not very intelligent or worldly. He racked his brain for a conversation starter. Caroline met his eyes once or twice, and sensing his shyness, she smiled at him sweetly, and then said, "Ies tells me you have been to the Riviera. What was France like?"

Soli breathed a deep sigh of relief, aware that he had been thrown a rope.

"The Riviera is beautiful. The beaches are perfect, and the weather is superb. Of course, I went with a group of boxers for a program, so I didn't get much of an opportunity to travel around. We didn't have that much spare time…."

"I've always wanted to see the famous boutiques there," Caroline revealed. "Did you see any of the beautiful homes there or meet any interesting people? It all seems so glamorous to me. I would love to travel there one day."

"Well, it is everything they say and more – as glamorous as in the movies," said Soli. "The men are wealthy, young, and handsome, and the women resemble starlets in their beautiful beach clothes. Everywhere I turned, it felt like I was encountering another Greta Garbo and Marlene Dietrich."

"Oh, so you find Marlene Dietrich and Greta Garbo glamorous, do you?" Caroline laughed flirtatiously. "Which one do you think is more talented?" she asked, her tone becoming more serious. She was genuinely interested in his opinion. She loved the movies, and once in a while, she treated herself to the Saturday evening film in the city. Caroline was passionate about the stories, the actors and actresses, and their magical screen worlds. She was hoping to find the same passion in Soli's voice.

"Greta was certainly very mysterious in *Flesh and the Devil*," Soli continued. "She is very beautiful and very sexy." He paused, and coyly added, "But nowhere near as mysterious or beautiful as you."

Caroline laughed awkwardly.

"Are you trying to flatter me?" she asked, thoroughly pleased at his compliment.

Soli gave her a shy, mischievous smile in response, then laughed along with her.

"I might be," he replied, with a lilt in his tone.

They marveled together at Charles Laughton's *Quasimodo* and Maureen O'Hara's *Esmeralda,* and talked at length about *Gone With the Wind*. Caroline confessed that movies were her way of escaping, if only for a brief time, the harsh realities of their world. It was liberating to transport oneself into another time, another place, another situation. Of course, this release was only temporary, and the moment the movie ended, reality prevailed.

"Yes, I know what you mean by that," affirmed Soli.

Caroline hoped that she had given Soli enough encouragement for him to ask to see her again. Perhaps they could see a movie together, since it was clear they had this hobby in common, but she saw from his demeanor that she would have to wait until he gathered the courage to ask her the question she was longing to hear. She watched him knit his long fingers together, as he composed himself. Finally, Soli asked, "Would you like to come out with me next Sunday morning?"

Caroline accepted the invitation with no hesitation.

When the evening came to a close, Caroline walked Soli to the door while Aaron and Ies followed along behind them. Ies was thrilled to see his sister so happy, but he was also troubled by the thought that their next meeting would be for far more serious reasons.

*

The following Sunday morning, Caroline woke up early. She had been eagerly waiting for this day. She frantically pulled out all of her clothing from the closet, and held each item against herself in front of the mirror. She wanted her first date with Soli at the zoo to be perfect, and she was determined to look her best. Finally, she pulled out an especially beloved dress, black and white with a soft embroidered blouse and bias cut skirt, from the closet. She always felt feminine and desirable in this dress, but today it would need to be ironed in order for her to look her best. She glanced at the clock near her bed and saw that she had only two hours left until she was supposed to be meeting Soli. There was still a great deal more to do.

Soli awoke at 6:15 A.M. that Sunday. He had not slept well in general since he met Caroline, and the previous night was no exception. Caroline dominated his thoughts entirely. He had been waiting impatiently for the day of their first date to arrive. He left his house at 7:00 A.M. and reached the Central station by 7:40. At eight, he boarded the train to Rotterdam and arrived in the city fifty minutes later. Though it was a bit of a distance, Soli decided to walk to Blijdorp. He berated himself for having neglected his morning exercises, and was determined to resume his walking, and what better opportunity than today? He was also frightfully early for his date, and needed to pass some time. He hoped that the walk would settle his nerves as well.

Soli arrived at the zoo's entrance at 9:40. It was still very quiet. Soli whistled to himself and tapped his foot gently on the ground while he looked around at the almost deserted zoo. He suddenly noticed Caroline crossing the street and walking toward him, and as he watched her, he swore he could feel his heartbeat quicken. She smiled and waved at him, and walked quickly across the street to where he was standing. They embraced and kissed each other on the cheek, as was the custom.

Caroline smelled of flowers, lily of the valley and linden. Soli took in her fragrance, the closeness of her body, and the soft texture of her clothing as she moved close to him. She was a lovely, statuesque woman, with warm hazel eyes and a graceful, long neck. She wore a strand of pearls and a set of pearl earrings, and almost no make-up, save for a touch of red on her lips. She smiled brightly as she said hello, and Soli was stunned by her beauty. He purchased two tickets at the entrance and took her hand in his.

They first walked towards the deer cages, each keeping up with the other in pace. Caroline stopped to look at the deer more closely. She loved deers. As they wandered leisurely around the zoo, Soli told Caroline about his work at the diamond exchange, and the enormous responsibility he had in carrying out his role. He also mentioned the sizeable wages he earned for his efforts. Caroline was enjoying listening to him talk; they did not run out of topics to discuss, and savored each moment of their discovery of one another. She was encouraged to hear him talk about his work – it meant he was serious in his intentions towards her. She was delighted to see that Soli was confident and ambitious in his plans for his future – a future he might possibly want her to share.

Caroline sold women's clothing in the French Bazaar, but it was work she did out of necessity. Her income helped support her six brothers and sisters, since her father, Moses, had been unable to work for quite some time, due to the recession. Caroline's mother, Henriette, had died the previous year, at the age of sixty-three. Caroline's situation at home was far from ideal; in fact it was miserable due to poverty and the extreme burden of caring for her siblings. Soli, with his possibilities for a new life, gave her a glint of hope. They sat under a shady tree and savored the still morning.

The zoo had only been open a few weeks, and it had not yet become a popular city spot; the young couple were glad of the privacy. They became so engrossed in their conversation that they did not notice how much time had passed. The morning wore on, and the zoo became crowded with visitors. Caroline looked at her watch and was surprised to see that it was already 2:00 P.M.

Caroline stood up, and Soli took her hand again; he led her to a café where they sipped coffee served with mounds of whipped cream and spiced ginger biscuits. Soli suspected that he was dangerously and helplessly in love with this beautiful girl. Caroline smiled at him as she savored her coffee. Surely, thought Soli, she must feel the same way. At 6:00 P.M., Soli took Caroline home.

Across the street from her house, Caroline thanked Soli for a wonderful day, then moved closer to him for an embrace. Their lips brushed momentarily and then their eyes met, still unsure about how the other felt, but obviously wanting the other to initiate a kiss. They giggled and separated, and Soli held on to her hand as she pulled away to cross the street to her door. He watched as she climbed the steps and waved from the doorway, then waited for her to close the door behind her before he started to head home.

*

Soli and Caroline's relationship blossomed as time passed. In January of the following year, Soli took Caroline to The Hague to visit the Binnenhof. He also took her to the Knight's Hall and knelt before her as if he were waiting for the ceremony. When she laughed at his playfulness, he proposed to her in earnest. She kissed him passionately and accepted. Their wedding ceremony took place on January 10, 1941. It was a small affair in Amsterdam, consisting mostly of close family members who were invited to toast the couple with a glass of champagne. The newlyweds went to The Hague after the festivities to a room in Hotel des Indes. There they celebrated their honeymoon, two young people who were very much in love.

Soli and Caroline Kanes in The Hague, 1942.
This is the only existing photograph of Soli Kanes

Chapter 2
Resisting the Germans

SOLI AND CAROLINE started their married life in an attic studio with a hidden extra room on the Uilenburgerstraat, in the heart of the Jewish district, right next to his father's house. The newlyweds decided to move to the studio because the rent was affordable and the apartment very comfortable. For the first time, Caroline felt as if she had her very own home, and she loved the space. She immediately set about decorating the apartment with plants and Delft plates. She worked at this away from the noise and demands of her brothers and sisters, and the often overbearing dictates of her father. She luxuriated in the knowledge that for the first time, she was able to make her own decisions.

But the most wonderful thing about being married was the love and affection lavished upon her by her new husband. She realized how delightful it was to be loved in this way. Living with her father and siblings presented too many hardships. There were always other people's needs to consider: food to be put on the table, brothers and sisters to dress, clean, feed, and look after. There was little time for affection in her family; each person focused their energies on making ends meet and struggling through the next crisis. The fact that Moses Nathan had been out of work for years did not do much to improve the situation. For the first time she could remember, Caroline was the center of attention in her own home. She savored every moment of this attention and blossomed under Soli's constant adoration.

Caroline and Soli loved to socialize in the neighborhood haunts. One of their favorite places was the Koco Ice Cream Parlor, owned by partners Ernst Cahn and Abe Kohn. Business boomed in the Koco, and the owners attracted people to their café with their Bohemian personalities and brilliant minds. Locals loved to come to the Koco to listen to Ernst's philosophical ideas and musings, and they enjoyed the charm and generosity of their hosts. Soli particularly admired Abe and Ernst, as they were Jewish refugees from Nazi Germany. Caroline would enjoy listening to the different discussions that took place in the Koco, where they would meet their group of friends. When Soli would meet with the members of the Defense League, Caroline participated in the conversations, and soon found her niche. She loved being involved in the League, as she could openly contribute her ideas and opinions, while at the same time enjoying the company of those around her. As well as being sociable and vivacious, Caroline often raised questions that provoked much thought, and steered the group towards more serious discussions.

Caroline felt like a different person since she married Soli. They were both so happy and in love, yet they could not dispel the fear and worry that bombarded them; the world was changing and for the worst. The pleasure and novelty that pervaded their married life was dampened by the knowledge that danger and uncertainty were lurking. Every week brought fresh, harsh decrees against the Jews; each week, Jewish citizens faced yet another restriction on his or her freedom, and another threat from the now commonplace roving groups of Dutch Nazi youth. The Koco was a natural haven for Caroline and Soli, even as the brutality within the Jewish neighborhoods escalated.

Jews were barred from cinemas and stores, and many shop owners were forced by the NSB to stop serving Jewish customers. The number of "Juden niet gewenst!" signs multiplied in the city, as the NSB went about enforcing the dictates of restriction. Because the Koco was owned and managed by Jews, the business itself could not be forced into excluding its Jewish customers, but it became a target of intense violence and anti-Semitic acts that plagued other such businesses in Holland. Ernst and Abe benefitted from their Jewish clientele, who protected them from the roving bands of anti-Semites, and in return they provided locals with a warm and cosy meeting place that was free of any negative associations of fear.

The beginning of 1941 saw the establishment of a Jewish ghetto in Amsterdam, the establishment of a Jewish Council, and the first punitive roundups and deportations. News of the violence against Jews, and those who protested the new dictates, travelled from places as far away as Utrecht, The Hague, and Arnhem. It filled the ice cream parlor and became the focus of every conversation in every neighborhood. In the Jewish districts of Amsterdam, people were being threatened and intimidated on a regular basis; some were even brutally beaten or killed. With every new report, Soli and his friends became increasingly anxious to take steps against the violence, so they organized themselves into Brigades, and met more frequently to discuss methods of resisting violence within their own neighborhoods. Soon, discussions became more heated, and were focused on the direct impact the Defense Brigades would have in their areas.

Eventually, Caroline stopped going to the Koco with Soli. She was unsure as to whether she still wanted to participate in these impassioned discussions. It was all too clear in her mind that the violence was steadily encroaching, and she questioned the wisdom in being directly involved in the Resistance. She wanted to focus her efforts entirely on her marriage with her new husband. Everything else seemed too frightening to contemplate. She did not want to live in constant fear of losing her husband to one of his secret, nightly patrols, but Soli was impatient to act. He went out to the Koco to meet with the Defense Brigades every night, and as time passed, he would return home later and later. He never spoke to Caroline about his discussions now. He tried to keep any of his own plans a secret from her, as he knew she was becoming increasingly nervous about his involvement.

One night Soli came home very late and found Caroline waiting up for him. She appeared agitated and was pacing around the apartment nervously.

"What is happening, Soli?" she asked, turning to face him.

He realized how frightening things must seem to her, and chose his words carefully. He spent the next hour explaining to her their plan of action, the work each of the Defense Brigades would do as the situation warranted. Soli spoke with fervor, but Caroline did not share in his excitement.

"I am afraid you will get hurt or killed," she said, envisioning the escalation of violence that would inevitably result. Caroline reflected on the current situation; a war was being waged, and her own people were in the firing line. It was against her nature to be passive when such pointed attacks were being levelled against Jews, but she feared that violent counterattacks would be counter-productive. Perhaps fighting was preferable to passivity, she concluded. She looked at Soli meaningfully and warned him not to let himself get arrested.

"I'll do my best," he said.

"And don't get yourself killed, either," she pleaded with him.

"If it happens, I'll make sure to take some of them along with me," said Soli, in an attempt to lighten her mood.

It didn't help, but at least it ended the conversation. He wrapped his arm around his wife and led her to their bedroom. Neither of them managed to sleep, both of them absorbed in their myriad of thoughts and worries, but they derived comfort from their proximity to one another. Soon the destruction of cafés, dance halls, restaurants, and shops were rampant in every Jewish neighborhood in Holland. The NSB was becoming methodical in its terrorism, advancing to any and all areas in an effort to destroy any place where there were Jews. The Dutch police made a valiant effort to act as peacemakers in these incidents, trying to convince Nazi groups to leave the neighborhoods and avoid creating confrontation. At first, their efforts were somewhat effective, but this soon proved to be unsustainable. Jews, non-Jewish neighbors, laborers, and supporters from other districts of Holland organized and protected themselves from NSB provocation, just as Soli and the Defense Brigades were trying to do. In some cases, the NSB would retreat, just as the police did; in other cases, it was only the police who would retreat, leaving that particular neighborhood to defend itself against the growing wrath of the NSB.

The violence persisted. Soli, Moshe Hamburg, and Jaap Praag patrolled the areas where the Dutch Nazis were present in their own neighborhood. They vigilantly watched the streets in the district. Soli exuded confidence. He and his friends were all young and strong, and his years of practice as a boxer gave him countless skills in strategy and self-defense. As a precautionary measure, he also carried a knife. He was aware of the danger of being attacked by a deadly weapon, and the knife was an insurance policy against any aggressors. When he and his troupe patrolled the streets, Soli would adopt the role of a predator on the hunt. He and the others worked together to be the most effective defensive team possible. Each "watch" had about forty-five other members, dispersed throughout the community so that they could cover a greater distance. They all remained within calling distance of one another, though, just in case anyone urgently required assistance.

On the night of February 11, the cold wind cut through Soli's clothing as he waited in the building shadows with Jaap and Moshe. They were well hidden, but could see everything that was happening in the streets around them. The streets were not yet empty; it was ten minutes past six, and there were still some people who had not yet come home from work. They could be seen walking purposefully in the direction of their houses, trying to dodge the wind and indeed, the NSB.

Soli watched an elderly couple walk towards their front door. The man put his arm protectively around his wife, and led her as quickly as possible past the people around them. He watched as the woman tried to move more quickly, responding to her husband's growing fear. Soli suddenly thought about Caroline, and hoped she was safely home from work herself. Caroline continued to work in the French Bazaar, selling clothes, even after she got married.

He pictured himself and Caroline as that old couple; for as long as he lived, he would continue to protect her. Thoughts of whether they would actually live long enough to reach old age haunted him, but he quickly banished them out of his mind. Now was not the time to let fearful ideas creep into his head. A loud screeching of tires jolted him out of his thoughts. Six cars stopped abruptly just a few feet away from the couple, and tens of NSB men emerged, brandishing clubs and knives and yelling at the tops of their voices. Immediately, the Defense Brigades went into action: Soli and his friends were the first to emerge from the shadows, but other groups of brigades quickly overpowered the shocked NSB, who had not envisioned any resistance.

The NSB was easily disadvantaged because of their lack of foresight, but Soli and his friends still found themselves locked in a violent struggle with the attackers they had thrown off guard. One of the thugs jammed his elbow into Soli's face, and he reeled from the pain. His cheekbone felt as if it had been crushed, but he came back at his attacker, smashing his fist into the man's face. He felt the thug's nose compress under his knuckles, and soon he was covered with the blood of his assailant. Samson Praag, Jaap's brother, wrestled with another attacker and let out a tremendous scream as a hunting knife was jabbed into his arm. Instantly, Soli and Hartog Hamburg, Moshe's cousin, jumped on Samson's attacker, and in a torrent of fear and adrenaline, they stabbed at the Nazi with their own knives. Samson managed to extricate himself and watched breathlessly as Soli and Hartog kept up their force, crazed and in terrible pain themselves.

Outnumbered, the other NSB members hurriedly dispersed. The sounds of whistles blowing grew in momentum as the Dutch police approached. Soli and Hartog realized that they were going to be caught attacking their assailant, who lay bleeding on the ground before them. Punch-drunk and heavily breathing, Soli hoarsely whispered, "We have to go, before anyone finds us…now!" They separated and ran off into the shadows, away from the approaching police. Covered in blood and exhausted, Soli limped home. It took all of his energy for him to find his way.

Caroline had just started cooking dinner; she was expecting Soli to be home from his tour of duty at ten o'clock. It was only a few minutes past eight when she heard a key turning in the door. She expected the worst and gasped as Soli stumbled into the house, his clothes and face covered with dried blood. She could see that he was hurt and ran for some towels and clean water. Soli was still in a state of shock.

"Caroline…Caroline," he mumbled, "I think we killed someone…." he said, trying to catch his breath.

"What happened?" Caroline demanded, vacillating between concern and anger, that he should have placed himself in such a dangerous predicament. "Tell me what happened to you tonight, Soli."

She removed his soiled clothing while he told her what he remembered of the fight. She cleaned his face with a warm washcloth and wrapped the sore knuckles of his right hand.

Soli mumbled absently until she finished cleaning him up, and put him in some clean, warm clothing.

"I don't know if the Nazi we stabbed is still alive," he said softly. "I'd better go and find the others and find out." Caroline could see he was not thinking clearly. Enough was enough. She would not tolerate this anymore; the time had to come to stop Soli from participating in further foolish incidents.

"Soli, you are not going anywhere tonight. It is too dangerous. The NSB and the police will be looking for someone who matches your description and is covered with blood, bruises and cuts. They will know you just came from a fight, and they will put two and two together very easily. You are better off meeting in the morning. Until then, you had better lay low."

The next morning, all the newspapers reported the skirmish on their front pages.

The NSB member that Soli had stabbed, a forty-five-year-old Hendrik Koot, was in critical condition at the hospital. There was a great deal of tension and hostility growing in the community as a result of the news. The NSB was itching to exact revenge, and the Jews readied to protect themselves from any kind of impending onslaught. It was clear to everyone that tension would only grow over the next few days – especially if Koot were to die in hospital of his wounds. In the meantime, Soli stayed home whenever necessary and tried to maintain a low profile in other ways.

At work at the diamond exchange, Soli learned that changes were scheduled to take place on-site, which would mean greater communication between the Nazis and the exchange. He received a note at work that Thursday, asking him to attend a meeting with the other workers in the great hall of the exchange.

He and Moshe arrived at the meeting ten minutes early to find the hall already filled with workers. When Abraham Asscher stepped up to the podium to give his address, the hall became silent. Asscher was a philanthropist who was known for his work before the war on the Committee for Special Jewish Affairs. He announced that a representative body, chaired by Professor David Cohen and himself, would be formed. It would include Mr. Voet, a former chairman of the Dutch General Diamond Workers' Union, and a butcher from the Jodenbreestraat called Quiros. The board would act as a liaison between the Jewish communities and the Nazi authorities so that violence from both sides could be avoided in the future. In the meantime, in light of the recent violent outbreaks in the community, Asscher insisted that all weapons held in Jewish hands be surrendered to the police.

Moshe and Soli exchanged looks of anger and dread, as they knew this would leave them and their community without means of self-protection. After leaving the meeting, they agreed that they should call their groups together for a meeting, so that they could discuss and plan anew in light of this development. On Friday, Hendrik Koot died from his wounds. The violence in the community continued to escalate as the Nazis began to exact

revenge against what they portrayed as the work of "terrorists." Violence
continued to surround Koot's death; his funeral was followed by outbursts
of attacks.

Even the Koco was vandalized. Its windows were smashed by a band
of NSB thugs who managed to bash in the café before the authorities inter-
vened and sent them away. Real trouble arrived on Wednesday, February
19, when a detachment of German soldiers surrounded the Koco. They
had been informed that this venue was a favorite meeting place for the
league members, whom they suspected of being in some way responsible
for Koot's death.

When Ernst saw the men in uniform, he was sure the NSB had returned. He tossed a bottle of ammonia gas at them, which exploded and
wounded several Nazis. They fired back at Ernst, who was assisted by
onlookers, but they proved to be no match against the superior Nazi forces.
The parlor was raided, but Ernst, Abe, and the rest of the men with them
ran out the rear exit and up to the roof of the adjoining building. Ernst and
Abe managed to escape, but the Nazis declared a curfew and arrested them
later that evening. Immediate reprisals were ordered after this incident: Abe
received a ten-year prison sentence, while Ernst was sentenced to death.
Abe died after he was deported, and Ernst was executed a few days later,
on March 3, 1941.

The following Saturday afternoon, the Nazis raided the Jewish quarter.
They cordoned off the entire area while they dragged people off the streets
and broke into homes, looking for Jews. Those who resisted were severely
beaten. Four hundred and fifty Jewish citizens were arrested and taken to
the square, Jonas Daniel Plein, where they were forced to run a gauntlet
through rows of policemen who beat them. They were then taken to an
internment camp and finally sent to Mauthausen. Over the next three
months, all would perish there. The Nazis were finally showing their true
colors, and were behaving in Holland in the same way as they had been in
Germany since 1933.

The Dutch citizens who witnessed the grotesquely violent raid were
indignant. Terrible as the sight may have been, it must surely have played
an important role as the catalyst for the creation of the Dutch Resistance
to the Nazi forces.

Chapter 3
The February Strike

SOLI AND CAROLINE mimeographed and distributed leaflets for a one-day strike to take place on February 25. The daylong shutdown was to be a protest against the growing Nazi aggression perpetrated against the Dutch Jewish community. Though the Dutch Communist party originally conceived of the strike, the idea was so popular that support for the plan grew throughout the city, tapping into a vein of anger against the now commonplace violence towards Jews. Other political parties and trades, who had been forced underground by the Nazis – such as the Social Democrats, patriots, municipal employees, and many of the organized labor in the metal and shipyards – supported the activities planned by the Communist party. They joined in the effort to present a unified, unbroken front of resistance. Even the Dutch police, who had to stand watch over the protest, refused to interfere with the proceedings. As the crowds grew in size, and the workings of the city's transit and manufacturing systems came to a complete and resounding halt, the Nazis were caught entirely unprepared. Such a strike was unprecedented in Europe, and they were at a loss to end such a display of unified resistance against their authority. Gerhard Boemcker, a bureaucratic aide to Seyss-Inquart, who was to represent him in his absence, could only request that the mayor of Amsterdam and the chief of Amsterdam's police force end the strike. In response, neither of these two officials would be pressed to take the action demanded by the Nazis against the oppressors; their responsibility was to protect their people. In frustration, the Germans placed SS men in Amsterdam to impose and enforce a curfew on the city. The protesters disbanded when they were forced to do so, but in defiance, people remobilized the next day with even more citizens of Amsterdam protesting the Nazi decrees. Now even the private sector's workforce supported the strike, and news of the growing numbers spread to other cities in Holland.

In Haarlem and Zandaam, citizens organized strikes of their own. It was becoming clear to the Nazis that the one-day strike had become a much more sustained and widespread protest. Nazi frustration with such open resistance grew more intense. When strikes spread to other areas, and the Amsterdam strike showed no signs of letting up, the Germans took steps to ensure that their forces would no longer tolerate the demonstrations. Soli and his friends were present in the crowds, protesting along with their neighbors. There was a great deal of camaraderie amongst all those present, and Soli felt proud to be Dutch, and lucky to be in Amsterdam where he could witness with his own eyes the tremendous strength of his countrymen.

As the second day of the strike wore on, though, heavily armed Nazi police and SS guards swarmed the streets in what were at first weak and implausible attempts to arrest the instigators of the strike. Such a united front was presented by the crowd that there was no way the Nazis would have been able to single out any one "instigator." Clearly, the Nazis were faced with an entire wall of people determined to act against the German authority.

Before long, however, Nazi frustration brought violence. They opened fire on the crowd, aiming their guns randomly at the sea of faces. Hundreds of people were wounded, and many protesters were killed. The crowds dispersed while those who were still able to flee sought shelter. Anyone caught by the Nazis was arrested, and many of the workers who took part in the strike ended up in concentration camps. The Nazi presence in the crowd, insurmountably deadly, finally put an end to their act of defiance. The Germans became even more determined to implement their anti-Semitic policies as a result of the strike's success. They realized that they would have to enforce their dictates far more vigorously in the future, and make a priority of curbing the Communist Party's activities, once and for all.

Most important, they would have to step up their own regulations within the Jewish communities themselves. The strike made two things clear: first, the Nazis would stop at nothing, not even outright aggression, to achieve their ends. Second, the Nazis could force the Dutch into submission, but they would never win support for their ideology.

Soli and Caroline argued frequently about the other's involvement in the resistance. Soli would try to keep Caroline from participating actively because he firmly believed that such warfare was a man's job. Caroline argued that she was under just as much threat from the enemy as any man was, and that she could actually be much more effective since women were not under the same suspicion as the men, and hence were not being watched as carefully by the Germans. She subtly pointed out that Soli had already been hurt once in his resistance work, and suggested that perhaps he should be a little more careful himself. In the end, they agreed to disagree. What mattered was that they were only concerned about the other's safety. Both of them knew that in such dangerous times, each of them would have to act to defend themselves. Both Soli and Caroline had to accept that they would both do whatever necessary, and they agreed to work in the Resistance together.

The most recent cause for concern was the speech that Abraham Asscher had given days earlier at the diamond exchange. The Germans had ordered the establishment of a Jewish representative body, and found Asscher, a diamond entrepreneur and philanthropist, along with Professor David Cohen, willing to chair this body. The Germans primarily wanted to establish this Jewish Council so that the existing Jewish Coordination Committee (JCC) would be eliminated. This committee had been created to overcome the fragmented and often divisive relationship that existed between the different branches of Dutch Jewry. The honorable Judge Lodewijk Visser, the recently suspended president of the high court who was inherently opposed to the idea of a special Jewish Council, had been the committee's chairman.

By the autumn of 1941, the Jewish council had succeeded in using its contacts with the German authorities to extend its influence and control to include all matters pertaining to the Jewish communities throughout Holland. Judge Visser remained adamant that cooperation with the Germans was the way to ruin. He insisted that the Dutch authorities should protect Jews of Dutch nationality; this was not to be achieved by specially created organizations that would imply a difference between Jews and Dutch citizens. So, in effect, he pointed out, this new Jewish Council worked hand in hand with the Germans in direct opposition to the policies of the JCC, which refused direct contact with the occupiers.

Many agreed that Asscher might have been well intentioned in his attempts to spare the Jews from their fate, but had made a grave error in trying to convince the Jews to surrender their weaponry to the Nazis. This would effectively create a distinction between the Jews and the rest of the Dutch in Holland – isolating Jews from the support and resistance that their fellow citizens were demonstrably willing to provide. It became clear to the members of the Resistance that they would need to distance themselves from the Jewish Council and work to strengthen their ties with other underground resistance groups. They already knew that the official institutions representing the Jewish community in Holland could no longer shield them from the new Nazi authority. In fact, it became more apparent each day that those institutions were being used for the disempowerment of the Jews; their only chance against becoming completely vulnerable was to unite their forces even more cohesively.

Just as Caroline and Soli had feared, the Nazis began to enact new laws every day, and imposed even more restrictive anti-Jewish laws that affected every aspect of their lives. Jews were no longer granted access to public parks and swimming areas, theaters, shops, and cafés. They were no longer permitted to work in the markets or maintain businesses in areas frequented by other Dutch citizens. They were forbidden to trade on the stock markets and were forced to register all their assets with Lippman-Rosenthal, a bank that the Nazis had seized from its original Jewish owners. Now that the Nazis had acquired it, all the financial affairs of the Jews could be monitored and controlled. The laws effectively isolated the Jews both socially and economically from their fellow Dutch citizens. They were left with little money, no means of earning a livelihood, and no place to turn to for help within the country. As the Nazis advanced their anti-Jewish measures, the Resistance increased its activity with equal force. It bombed a club frequented by Nazi marine officers, which wounded several of them.

In the beginning of June, 1941, Samson Praag and Isaac Kanes were accomplices in blowing up the Luftwaafe telephone exchange at Schiphol Airport, causing a minor, but disruptive, setback to the German operation. Several soldiers were injured, sparking an even more vicious anti-Jewish retaliation. The Nazis let loose with a series of raids in the Jewish districts, during which hundreds were rounded up and sent directly to the Mauthausen concentration camp. The increased ferocity of Nazi anti-Semitism indicated their ultimate plan of incarcerating, and possibly annihilating, all the Jews in Holland. The Dutch were horrified and appalled to witness the spectacle of their neighbors and friends being rounded up and taken away to an unknown fate. As the harshness of the occupation grew, so did Dutch unrest and resentment towards the Germans. The atrocities committed by the Nazis gave birth to several more resistance groups comprised of outraged Dutchmen, who organized and facilitated the hiding and sheltering of Dutch Jews, known as *onderduikers* (underdivers). These brave individuals began by recruiting relatives, friends, and neighbors to join the first resistance organization.

The dangers were exceptionally high: captured members of the resistance were usually shot or sent to concentration camps. The primary anti-Nazi activity started at this time with the aid of the Social Democrats and Catholic youth leagues.

Chapter 4
Celebrating Deliverance

O N APRIL 14, Caroline and Soli prepared themselves to celebrate the "Seder" Passover meal with Soli's family. They were very excited at the prospect of spending their first Passover as a married couple with all of Soli's family. Soli had one brother, Maurits, who was married to Rebecca, and one sister, Anna, who was married to Ezechiel Bruinvelds. They looked forward to the occasion like any young couple in love, carefully selecting their clothes and helping the other polish their appearance.

Caroline had set aside a special white suit with saddle stitching detail along the hems, to wear on this spring day. She took an hour to style her hair and carefully applied a subtle amount of makeup. Soli put on his best suit and deliberated over the appropriate tie. Caroline helped him knot his tie while looking straight into his light green eyes, and they laughed together. She stood back to take stock of her husband in his finery and smiled while Soli did the same. They each admired the other, standing in their best clothing, ready to meet the family together.

"I am going to wear the Shalimar you gave me for my birthday," announced Caroline. She dabbed a little to her wrist and held it up to Soli for him to sample.

"Hmm," he sighed appreciatively, "you smell delicious, like a flower."

The couple left their apartment, hand in hand, and walked next door to the Kanes house. Soli's parents greeted them at the door where they all exchanged kisses. Levie Kanes, Soli's father, marvelled at the beauty of his daughter-in-law, exclaiming, "You are stunning!" as he kissed her.

"Now I know where Soli learned to be such a flatterer!" replied Caroline, smiling at her father-in-law.

The house was filled with the seductive aromas of the feast, and as this was such an important holiday in the Jewish tradition, Soli's mother, Esther, had laid out their finest Passover accessories on the table. It was covered in a crisp white damask cloth, and each of the ten settings was set with gold-rimmed porcelain Bavarian dishes. The cut crystal glassware made the table glisten against the soft spring light. The beautifully laid table and the inviting smells were deliciously enticing, and the family took their seats at the table, eager for the Seder to begin. Once they had all gathered, Levie stood at the head of the table, and everyone rose while he recited the Kiddush, the blessing of the wine. They then proceeded to read the Haggadah. Soon it was time for the youngest child to ask "*mah nishtanah*," the traditional four questions.

Esther, the daughter of Soli's brother Maurits, was the youngest child present who was able to recite this portion of the Haggadah. She stood ready to ask the questions while the room grew silent around her. She stood proudly in the new pink lace dress that her mother, Rebecca, had sewn for her, and her tiny voice started, "*Ma nishtanah halaila hazeh mikol halailot?*" ["Why is this night different from all other nights?"]

Everyone was amazed at how well Esther sang the questions. They smiled at her encouragingly while she was singing. When she finished her part, everyone rushed forward with compliments and kisses. Then Levie continued with the proceedings. He paused every couple of pages to explain the meaning of the Exodus from Egypt, and to relate how God had split the Red Sea, allowing the Jews to cross to safety.

"We could sure use Moses to liberate us from these Nazis," Maurits commented. "There's plenty of sea around us to accommodate them all."

"I'll say amen to that," Soli quietly replied.

Levie blessed the second cup of wine, and then the time came for everyone to wash their hands. He broke the matzo and served it with bitter herbs, passing the dishes around the table. The bitter herbs were eaten to remind everyone present of the embittered times their forebears had endured in Egypt. When Levie finished, the meal would begin. Despite the economic restrictions imposed on the Jews, Esther had managed to prepare a sumptuous meal. She had saved money whenever she could, and had been diligent in her aim to serve chicken for the meal. Once she had all the ingredients at her disposal, she worked creatively to concoct new and tantalizing recipes. She worked efficiently and methodically, preparing the meal's courses days in advance. As hors d'oeuvres, she served a rich chopped liver, followed by a hearty matzo ball soup. She spent hours finding the right herbs and spices to season the chicken stock. Everyone gushed over the rich flavors of the dishes, the elegance of the table, and the warm conversation the dishes inspired. The main course consisted of stuffed chickens served with potato knishes. For dessert, Esther had prepared an appelmousse from fresh apples and honey. This year, the feast was doubly appreciated, because nowadays, such items were so scarce. The Seder felt surreal; in the face of such hardship and danger, the Kanes family were gathering and celebrating, in festive spirit, the Exodus from Egypt. They entertained thoughts in their heads of a contemporary Exodus, which could rescue them from the Nazi threat.

As Caroline talked warmly with her sisters-in-law, Anna and Rebecca, Soli enjoyed a Cuban cigar that his father had saved for him just for this occasion. He was careful to show his father that he knew the cigar was of excellent quality, and Caroline remembered he had mentioned the length of the ash as proof of his appreciation.

As the Seder continued with the singing of the traditional songs, Caroline thought to herself that this was one of the most enjoyable evenings she had ever spent. In her own family, she had never experienced such warmth and affection. Caroline maintained a very close relationship with her siblings, but her father was always a very reserved and awkward character. As the voices rose around her, she joined in, finally feeling as though she were part of a loving family. Albeit only for a few hours, the family were able to forget the decaying reality of their lives in Holland. The Seder night, with its message of redemption and deliverance, had renewed their faith and ignited hope.

However, that restored faith was short-lived. Life soon turned even more bleak. On April 29, the Nazis introduced the most drastic of their decrees, Decree 13, which forced all Jews to wear the yellow star. The Jews in Poland and Germany had already been forced to wear such identification for some time. The decree stated that the word "*Jood*" (meaning Jew) had to be sewn over the left breast of all outer clothing. Failure to comply with the decree would result in a six-month jail sentence and a fine of a thousand guilders.

The yellow stars made the members of the Jewish community highly identifiable and extremely vulnerable: it was now much easier to identify a Jew, and in turn, arrest him. Once again, however, many of the Dutch gentiles were outspoken in their solidarity with the Jewish people. The *De Volk* newspaper printed 300,000 paper stars with the inscription "Jews and non-Jews are one," for their readers to wear in protest. But the Nazis would not tolerate any insubordination: twenty-three students of Leiden University were sent to Amersfoort concentration camp for wearing the protest stars.

Soli and Caroline had both been forced out of work, and as a result, they found themselves in difficult economic straits. With no income and no prospects, Soli and Caroline tried to think of new ways to bring in money. Soli's sister, Anna, her husband Ezechiel, and their baby Kalman, had already moved in with Soli and Caroline in an effort to pool their diminishing resources. The four of them brainstormed for ideas for a small business; they had to find some way of surviving. With their meager savings combined, they had enough to start a small production company making orthopedic soles. They could prepare the merchandise at home, and Caroline would distribute their product to retailers. Anna was to look after the chores in the household and tend to the baby, while Caroline tried to sell their product to clients. The idea was a good one except for the fact that Jewish trade was limited to exchange with other Jews (another of the Nazi edicts). Caroline could distribute the product to the overwhelmingly poverty-stricken Jewish-owned businesses. But Jews all over Holland had lost their possessions, and they were stripped of their right to work. Jewish businesses were being driven into bankruptcy, and no one had any money to buy the product. It became overwhelmingly clear to all that there was no money to be made.

In their desperation, Caroline and Soli decided to move to The Hague, where there was less intervention from the Nazis, and in turn, a greater chance of generating business. Also, the Jews in The Hague were not concentrated in a ghetto.

Soli found a reasonable flat on Hoowijk Plein and the family moved to The Hague. They were just beginning to settle into their new life when Caroline suspected that she may be pregnant. It had been two months since she had last had her period, and she was worried. She went to see Dr. Moskowitz, and after taking a battery of tests, he called to confirm her suspicions. Never had she felt such a mixture of joy and fear. She knew Soli would be overjoyed, but she also knew they would have to make some radical changes in their lives because of the baby.

As Caroline suspected, Soli was overjoyed to learn he would be a father. He shouted out and danced around their tiny apartment, lifting Caroline up in the air, causing her to shriek and laugh. He caught her in his arms for a long, deep kiss.

As they chatted excitedly about the prospect of being parents, their thoughts became more sombre. What kind of world were they bringing their child into? Caroline and Soli considered their options; they discussed the possibility of emigrating to America, where Caroline's uncle, Bram Haag, had been living since 1928. Nothing concrete had been decided, but they both agreed that escaping from Holland was probably the wisest move. They would need to get the necessary papers, illegally, of course, as they were sure that travel would be restricted as well. They also had to find some way of paying for their trip. If they could somehow find a way to leave Holland, Soli and Caroline reasoned, Uncle Bram would surely help them settle in America.

Caroline and Soli worked at their plans, and each day brought them closer to the realization of their dreams for a better life for themselves and their unborn child. But on the fifth of August, everything changed for Caroline: Soli was detained in the street by Nazi thugs and was sent to the Westerbork labor camp. The next months were particularly hard on Caroline; not only was she pregnant, but she was alone. This feeling of isolation was compounded by the growing list of family members sent off to concentration camps. Her brother, Wolf Nathan, and his wife, Betsy, were among the unlucky ones who were rounded up and deported. Caroline was relieved to learn that they had left their baby, Haim, in Rotterdam with a Christian family. Her other brothers Aaron and Bram, and her sisters Betsy and Elizabeth, had all been sent to labor camps. When she heard that Soli's brother and sister-in-law, Maurits and Rebecca Kanes, had been sent to concentration camps with their two children Esther and Barend, Caroline understood that the horror stories were not just some nightmare;

they were now reality. For the first time, she considered the possibility that she may not survive the Nazi occupation, and the thought of being sent to a concentration camp sent shivers down her spine. She did not know whether Soli would ever see his new baby or whether she would ever see her husband alive again.

Ies made an extra effort to stay close to Caroline now that she was alone and pregnant, making sure she had everything she needed: adequate food, shelter, clothing, and encouragement – everything that was within Ies's power to provide. He was determined to circulate freely in order to continue providing for Caroline; He refused to wear the yellow star and took his chances. This allowed him a certain amount of anonymity in the world, so that he could continue to be active in the Resistance with the few friends who had managed to escape arrest. Since wearing the star made him a target of Nazi hatred, he had decided that being inconspicuous was the only effective way to sabotage the Nazi effort. He needed to stay out of danger at least until Caroline gave birth, and then he could make his own plans for the future. In the late afternoon of January 24, 1943, Caroline felt the first pangs of childbirth, and knew her labor had begun. Ies would be home at 6:00 P.M. for his dinner, so she knew she had to wait a couple of hours until she could go to the hospital. Finally, Ies returned to find Caroline sitting down on the floor, doubled over in pain, and realized that the time had come. He hurriedly prepared for them to leave, and rushed Caroline to the hospital.

"Are you going to stay with me in the hospital until the baby's born?" she asked him, half-hoping he would answer yes.

"I won't be able to, Caroline," he answered softly. Caroline heard in Ies's voice a sense of determination, as if he was resolved in his mind, and could not be swayed. She had an odd feeling that she would not be seeing her brother again for a long time. She suspected that something was not quite right.

"I'm leaving with some friends for France, early tomorrow morning," Ies said. "I'm going to fight with the Maquis."

Caroline tried to stay composed, even though she was in an increasing amount of pain and faced her own grave uncertainties about the future. She looked at her brother, whose clear eyes and determination seemed so strong. She wished she knew what to expect of the future and where she could find Soli. She knew she had to take one step at a time. The first task was to deliver the baby, and go on from there.

"Clientje," said Ies, using his sister's nickname, "try not to worry. Be strong and look after your baby."

He kissed her softly, picked up his bag, and left. It would be a very long time before Caroline would see her brother again.

After the initial ordeal of childbirth, Caroline revelled in the joy of being a mother. But she noticed that although it was normal for babies to cry, her baby, Levie, howled inconsolably, as though in great pain. Dr. Cohen hurriedly examined the baby and diagnosed that he had kidney stones, and that an operation was needed immediately. Cohen would use the operation, and the baby's extended recuperation time, to prevent Caroline from being shipped out of the hospital to the labor camps. The operation went ahead without any complications, and the baby recuperated slowly. But Cohen was determined to keep Caroline in hospital for as long as he could, using the baby's recuperation time as a plausible excuse. Eventually, not even Cohen's desire to be near to Caroline could justify her extended stay. On April 12, 1943, Caroline was finally discharged. She and her baby were accompanied to the train station, where she was told they were to be sent to Westerbork to be reunited with Soli. At first, she felt anxious to see Soli again, but she could not help but feel dread and a gnawing sense of fear at what would lie in store for them.

It was clear to Caroline that a newborn would be of little use in a labor camp. She would need to think of some way to keep her Levie out of the camp, where he would certainly meet instant death. The train stopped at the Utrecht station, where she could see hordes of people boarding the already crowded train. Caroline stood near a window on the train, where she could see nurses climbing aboard. Suddenly, an idea formed in her mind, and she stepped away from the window. She would have to act quickly....

Chapter 5
The Baby in the Basket

GERRIT VAN DER PUTTEN had just finished his twelve-hour shift as a Dutch police constable. He was formerly of the Koninklijke Marechaussee, the Royal Constabulary, established by King Willem the First in 1814 as the Monarchy's elite police force. Until 1940, the constabulary had been an organization distinguished for serving with various police departments throughout Holland, as well as with the armed forces. Gerrit was very unhappy with his current predicament: his family, including his father and grandfather, had served with honor in the ranks of the Royal Constabulary, and since the age of ten, it had been his dream to continue the family tradition by joining the Koninklijke Marechaussee. But since the Nazi uprising, the Marechaussee had been transformed into a regular constabulary force, performing day-to-day police work under the supervision of Nazi forces. Nazi sympathizers had replaced many of Gerrit's superiors, and some of his colleagues were stationed at Westerbork, guarding the labor camp.

Gerrit dreaded the possibility of being stationed to a similar location. He had heard horror stories of unconscionable acts from his peers; stories about the treatment of the Jews, who were packed into shoddy trains as if they were livestock. They were made to travel for three or four days at a time without fresh air, food or drink, or bathrooms. He had also personally witnessed a growing number of atrocities, such as the implementation of the new edicts, which restricted and targeted the Jews. He knew that soon he would be asked to commit the very same acts of violence. To ease his feelings of helplessness, and assuage his anger at the injustices he saw all around him, he decided to join the Dutch Underground. As a police officer, he was invaluable to the Resistance as a "pair of eyes" who could watch the Nazis closely while at work. He could only tolerate working in the police force if he somehow took advantage of his position there to assist the Resistance.

Gerrit had been informed that a small group of nurses had been allowed to board the train in order to treat the babies and the sick patients. "The Germans still want to impress us with their humanity," he'd muttered to himself bitterly. Yet another trainload of women and children were gathered at the station, forced to embark upon a journey from which many, Gerrit knew, would never return.

He smoked as he watched these poor unsuspecting wretches, dressed in what seemed to be rags and holding the last of their possessions close to their chests. Gerrit could not recall ever seeing such poverty-stricken people before, in such a state of indignity. He could hear the anguished cries of children as their mothers were informed they were being sent to a labor camp. Mothers clung to their babies in desperation, realizing how useless a small child would be in a camp where they would all be expected to "labor." They knew what this meant for the fate of their children.

Gerrit put out his cigarette and approached the train car nearest to him. On the other side of the train, Dutch police were busy directing a group of about thirty children and their parents onto the train, accompanied by several nurses. Gerrit recognized many of the nurses who were active in the Resistance, and spotted Grietje Verduin as she entered the railway car. Observing that the police were occupied herding the new passengers onto the train, she proceeded into the railway car, where several babies lay unattended in a corner. She examined the tiny infant closest to her and noticed a tiny scar on his right hip. Without saying a word, she picked up the baby and hid him in her basket of gauze and wound dressings. She quickly got off the train, placed the basket into Gerrit's arms, then turned around and allowed herself to blend into the crowd, wanting to be as inconspicuous as possible. The last Grietje saw of the baby, he was in Gerrit's arms as he disappeared into the shadows of the nearby buildings.

Gerrit realized that the basket contained a baby, and immediately snapped to attention. Quickly, he moved away from the train and retreated back into the shadows. Despite the hammering of his heart, Gerrit tried to act as normal as possible with his cargo, so as not to draw attention to himself. The whistle blew and the train pulled out of the station before Gerrit allowed himself to catch his breath.

He had to think fast: he would exit from the gate behind the buildings guarded by his colleagues. Not all of the other policemen were "trustworthy" these days, so he knew he had to be extremely cautious. He spotted Officer Hank Janssen at the gate, and felt a sudden surge of relief. Hank and Gerrit had known each other for a long time; Hank would never question why he was carrying a basket on his way home from work. Gerrit composed himself and took a deep breath before walking towards Hank, while holding the basket close to him. He saluted Hank, before continuing on his way. Hank saluted Gerrit back and watched him walk away. Gerrit forced a smile on his face as he walked towards his bike.

"I must be working too hard – I forgot my laundry yesterday!" he announced, motioning to the basket. Hank grinned politely, and immediately returned to his other duties.

Gerrit tied the basket firmly to the back of his bike, as if it truly were just filled with clothing, then quickly rode away. He knew of a contact address where he could go. He pedalled there, parked his bike, and rang the bell. Joop Wortman opened the door and let Gerrit in. Joop was a taxi driver, whose role it was to hand the baby over to a courier in The Hague. He told Joop about the baby, who complimented him for his fast work. Gerrit opened the basket so that he and Joop could take a look. Inside, they found a dark-haired baby, covered in only a diaper and the little blanket provided by the hospital. He still had his identity bracelet on his arm. "Levie Kanes, 25-1-43," read Gerrit out aloud. "Name and date of birth. I guess we have a baby with a biblical name," said Joop, looking at the wicker basket and smiling. "Remember, Moses in Exodus was also saved in a similar basket."

Geritt replied, "Yes, that's true."

"You have done very well," Joop praised Gerrit. "I will take care of little Levie now, but thank you for acting so diligently!"

Gerrit beamed. On his way home, he rehearsed the proud story he would tell his family about his efforts to save this beautiful baby in the basket.

Chapter 6
Father Verhoeven

THEO VERHOEVEN, born on September 17, 1907, was one of seven children born to Piet Verhoeven, the owner of a small café in the marketplace of Uden, a small town near Veghel in the southern province of Brabant. After finishing sixth grade, Theo was sent to the St. Willebrord Mission House in Uden. He had wanted to become a missionary ever since the elder bishop Pacificus Bos from Borneo visited them in Uden. He was enthralled by the stories the bishop told, and from that moment on he knew what he wanted to become. He finished his state exams in Utrecht with that goal in mind.

Theo pursued his goal to become a missionary and at the age of nineteen, enrolled in Helvoirt to complete his studies as a novice. For the next five years he continued studying at the theological school for higher studies in Tetering near Breda. He graduated in 1933 and was ordained into the priesthood. He was disappointed when instead of allowing him to go on a mission, as he had always envisioned, he was posted to a teaching job in Uden. He was then sent to the University of Utrecht in 1934, but after two years of studies, took ill and spent the next two years recuperating from his sickness. He was then allowed to continue his university studies in the classics and received his doctorate, cum laude, in 1940.

Once again, Theo returned to Uden as a teacher where he continued working until November 1941, when the invading German troops seized the mission for their personal use at the nearby airport in Volkel. The priests were given shelter in Veghel, where they occupied several buildings that were factories known as the Blue Kei. The Fathers became known as the Fathers of the Blue Kei.

Theo Verhoeven gave about twenty lessons a week at the Blue Kei in Christian philosophy, and was invited to move in with his sister and brother-in-law, Cor and Marie van de Nieuwenhof-Verhoeven on the Hezelaarstraat 26. Father Verhoeven was a Catholic priest with strong conviction and principles. Ever since the Nazis occupied Holland in 1940, he had done his best to maneuver around Nazi pressure. He hated their intentions and was vocal in his disapproval of the Nazi occupation. He was discreet, however, about his underground activities, and was associated with others in the Church who shared his opinions and plans, such as Father Titus Brandsma, a priest and journalist, who originated from Friesland. He was also the spokesman for the Dutch bishops for the freedom of the Catholic press. He had obtained his doctorate at the Gregorian University and lectured in the seminary while writing and publishing journal articles. During the 1930s, he had become well known as the rector of the Catholic University of Nijmeegen and as the chaplain of the Catholic journalists.

When the Nazis occupied Holland, they demanded that Father Brandsma dismiss all Jewish children from Catholic schools. Having protested as far back as 1935 against the Nazi policy towards the Jews in Germany, Brandsma refused to yield to the pressure of the Gestapo in Holland. He also urged the editors of Catholic newspapers to refuse to publish Nazi propaganda. Brandsma's act of defiance resulted in him being thrown into prison at Amersfoort, before he was transferred to Dachau, where he died, on July 26, 1942.

Father Brandsma's death left a deep impression on Theo; now, more than ever, he was determined to emulate Brandsma by continuing in the struggle against Nazism. Theo was among the Catholic clergymen who wrote and signed a telegram to Seyss-Inquart declaring their disagreement at the imminent deportations of the Jews. The telegram stated that the Nazi policies ran counter to the divine commandments of justice and charity. They ended their message with a call for all Catholic and Protestant clergymen in the country to preach from the pulpit against the Nazi war machine, instructing every parishioner to perform one's actions in the light of God.

It was a serious protest, which could turn the hearts of the occupied Dutch permanently against the Nazis, instilling in them a burning desire to get rid of the Nazis from Holland, once and for all. Seyss-Inquart was so certain of the damaging impact of that protest that he responded with a devastating threat of brutality: should they go ahead with their protest, he would no longer respect the protected status granted to baptized Jews by the Nazis. He would imprison everyone with Jewish roots, regardless of their chosen religion, and step up the activity the churches had declared abhorrent. Fearing they would endanger even more lives with their protest, the Protestant pastors considered their position carefully and backed down, but that did not stop Theo and his fellow clergymen from preaching the Church's opposition to the deportations that were widespread throughout Holland.

But soon enough, the Nazis carried out their threats, arresting any Jew who had converted to Catholicism, and swiftly sent them to their deaths. As a result of this decree, SS officers arrived at the Carmelite Convent at Echt, and arrested Edith Stein, then known as Sister Teresa Benedicta of the Cross, and her sister Rosa, and sent them to Amersfoort prison. From there they were transported to Westerbork, and finally, to Auschwitz, where they were sent to the gas chambers on August 9, 1942.

Sister Teresa's martyrdom became renowned throughout the clergy, inspiring Theo and many others to work against the Nazis at whatever cost. Father Theo was a great admirer of Sister Teresa. He had attended several of her earlier conferences and read many of her ingenious works, specifically, *Ways of Knowing God* and her two-volume translation of St. Thomas's work, *The Symbolic Theology of the Areopagite*. He felt a philosophical common bond with the sister, and admired her for the way he heard that she had treated her fellow prisoners. She was always calm and composed, and used her soothing demeanor to comfort and console the women and the children. She washed and groomed them, and ensured they were fed. Her experience as a volunteer at the military hospital many years earlier, where she had devotedly cared for soldiers suffering from dysentery, typhus, and cholera, now served her well. After the blow of losing Sister Teresa, Theo felt that he had to do everything in his power to save his fellow human beings. As if intended by heaven that Theo follow Sister Teresa's example, Theo heard from Arnold Hoogenhoff about two Jewish refugees who were in need of a safe place to live. Arnold had been harboring them for a few days, but the time had come to find them an asylum.

Arnold Hoogenhoff and his wife Paula were well known in Veghel. Paula and Arnold were considered to be among the first Nazi resistance members in Holland. Paula was born in Borken, in western Germany, and had been living in Veghel since her marriage to Arnold in 1930. They owned a small bookstore with a lending library, called Arnold's Books, in the Molenstraat. Even prior to the German invasion of Holland in 1940, Paula had been helping her brother in Germany smuggle Jews out to Holland. Arnold was influenced by his brother-in-law's heroic actions, and was inspired to help in the cause.

As the Nazis were invading Holland, a German couple, Rabbi Lokker and his wife, arrived at Arnold and Paula's door, seeking refuge. Arnold brought the couple to Piet van Hamont, who was willing to hide them. The saddle roof on the van Hamont house had a double wall: from the outside, there was nothing suspicious about this wall, but it had a secret door that led to part of the attic where the refugees could hide whenever danger presented itself. The rabbi and his wife spent most of the war with the van Hamonts. Paula and Arnold made certain that the Lokker's had everything they needed.

Because of the delicate and extremely dangerous nature of their resistance activities, Paula and Arnold were very careful about whom they took into their confidence, but eventually, Arnold decided to confide in Father Theo Verhoeven. Arnold told him that he was looking after a Jewish couple that was temporarily staying with Piet van Hamont. Arnold requested that Theo meet the couple, in the hope that he would be encouraged to aid other refugees in the future. Theo was extremely impressed by the rabbi and his wife, and Arnold wanted to know if Theo could find a home for another Jewish refugee. He asked if he could send a courier to assist Theo in his work.

Theo's first thoughts turned to the letter that the bishops had sent out to all the churches, protesting against the persecution of Jews. The letter, which stated the gross injustice of anti-Semitism, was a very brave move on the part of the church in Holland, but it was a far cry from decisive action, from adhering to the law of Christ, regardless of personal risk, as Father Brandsma had done. Theo desperately wanted to be effective in his resistance against such brutality. He thought very carefully about the possible ramifications of being involved in this way. The risks were great, and he was truly frightened. He knew that if he were caught harboring a fugitive evading the work draft to serve in Germany, the fugitive would be sent to work and he would be dismissed. But if he were caught harboring a Jewish refugee, the Nazis would arrest everyone involved, along with their families, and send them all to the concentration camps. Despite his fear of the potential dangers, he accepted them anyway. This development was the birth of the Hoogenhoff-Verhoeven Underground Organization.

Several days later, Dora Matthijssen, a courier, arrived from Amsterdam. Dora was a young Jewish woman in her twenties who resisted Nazi cruelty, and refused to live her life in hiding. She put her life at risk every day in order to help other Jews. At this particular time, she was trying to find refuge for a fifty-year-old woman who was recently ordered to present herself for labor in the East. Theo rode from farm to farm Wednesday afternoon, but to no avail; people were only willing to take in non-Jewish Dutch draft evaders. The next day, when he was free from teaching, he cycled around, looking and praying for a solution to present itself. When he crossed the bridge at St. Oedenrode, he learned about a farmer whose wife had become bedridden. He was in dire need of help for his children and in his farm, and was willing to take in the Jewish woman as long as she had good false identity papers. Grateful for the strength of his faith, and for the opportunity to help both the family and the Jewish refugee, Theo made the necessary arrangements.

News of his work spread, and an increasing number of Jewish *onderduikers* arrived just from Amsterdam. They came by train, where they would transfer in Boxtel, and descend at Veghel. There they found Arnold's Books, a safe house where they could find temporary safety. If the store was empty, Dora would lead the refugees up the stairs to the attic. There was a shortwave radio for receiving forbidden messages and a table for emergencies, where false identity papers could be made. Paula Hoogenhoff, who was German herself, received many German army personnel in her living room. They would come to the Bon Café, which was part of the bookshop, to relax and play chess or cards. No one would ever have suspected that just one floor above them, there were Jews hiding out.

Arnold was well suited to his work; his excellent memory enabled him to have on the tip of his tongue all of the names of the refugees and hiding places. It was Dora's role to move the refugees from place to place, to avoid suspicion or betrayal. If Dora or other couriers were ready to send a refugee over, Arnold would receive such messages in the post as, "I have here for your store an old edition of *The Little Johannes*, quite an old edition, at least fifty years old, with its cover in decent shape," or some other encoded way of transmitting the information.

"The inside of the book is in good shape" meant a female refugee; "slightly stained inside" indicated a male. Theo would also pass by the store window to see if there was a garden dwarf placed among the books. Its presence indicated, "Come in, there is work for you to do."

Soon a new courier arrived on the scene, named Gre van Dijk. She would accompany the people who came from the Den Haag-Leiden region. Mr. Oskam, who was the director of a company supplying food for cattle, and resided in Veghel, infiltrated her into the group. Mr. Oskam was in an excellent position, as he maintained a friendly relationship with the farmers; he himself also hid refugees. After Gre arrived, another courier from Den Haag known as "Tante Zus," was put in touch with Father Verhoeven.

On the evening of April 12, 1943, Theo passed by the bookstore and noticed the dwarf. He learned about the baby, Levie Kanes, who was saved by the Dutch policeman, and caught the next train to Utrecht.

Father Theo Verhoeven, Veghel, 1947

Chapter 7
Tante Zus

IN DRUTEN, on July 16, Helena Hogeveen gave birth to a baby girl. She and Nicolaas Pare, her husband, first held their daughter, Henrica Maria, when she entered the world that night. They contemplated all the things that new parents consider when they first hold their child in their arms. They anticipated the great accomplishments their daughter would achieve, and how beautiful she looked sleeping peacefully in their arms. But never in their wildest dreams could they have predicted what lay in store for Henrica.

Henrica's earliest memories were from Nijmeegen, where her family settled in 1899. The city thrived then, and her father took advantage of the booming economy to become a brick manufacturer. Henrica had led a sheltered and privileged childhood, filled with many happy hours of playing with her brother and other children from neighboring families. As well as being a contented and energetic child, she was also exceptionally brilliant and gifted. By the time she was in fourth grade, she was drawing and sketching at every opportunity. She would sketch the children around her and her surroundings. Henrica had the most fun when she was alone; she could absorb the people around her, and called on her skills as an artist to give animation and depth to her drawings. As a gift for her tenth birthday, her parents bought her a bicycle, giving her a sense of freedom and adventure she had never been allowed before. She rode her bike to school every day, and on Sundays, she and her older brother Nicolaas would take a picnic basket and ride to the villages just outside the city. There they would spend hours, as Henrica sketched the world around her: grass, trees, animals, people. She never grew tired of drawing and always found new excuses for these trips away, where she could concentrate on the activities she loved the most – riding her bike with her brother and drawing for hours on end.

As she got older, it was clear to Henrica that she was born to be an artist. She wanted to focus her efforts on painting, and she sought out the best painters and teachers to guide her in her ambition. In 1919 she was accepted to the Acadamie Voor Beeldende Kunsten in The Hague, which was considered to be one of the most prestigious art schools in Holland. She took up residence in a women's dormitory in The Hague and prepared for her life as an artist. She decided to take a professional name, and signed her paintings "Ru Pare," because the name Ru was easy to pronounce and remember. It became a popular nickname for her as her work gained recognition.

In the dormitory, Ru met Theodora Versteegh, an accomplished, thirty-year-old concert singer. The two women became instant friends. Ru was drawn to Theodora's exuberance, and the warmth of her character, and the two were to remain friends for the remainder of their lives. Ru flourished at the academy, where her work became increasingly original and prolific. She held her first exhibition during her first year at the school, and was one of a small group of women to exhibit their work. Ru studied under Willem van Konijnenburg, who saw much promise in her abilities and encouraged her development.

Ru and her list of admirers and friends continued to grow. She counted many artists she met at school among her friends, including Chris Lebeau, a commercial artist known for his work that appeared on the country's postage stamps. Ru also became connected with Jan Toorop, who helped her professionally through his work at a famous gallery, where he would often exhibit her paintings. One of the more provocative pieces she created at this time garnered much attention when the *Haagsche Courant*, the local newspaper, printed a copy of the painting along with a review of the exhibit. The publicity focused the attention of the artistic community on Ru's work, and she was invited to join the Amsterdam Group of Artists, as well as The Hague Group of Artists.

Theodora and Ru decided to share a house together in The Hague, and they found a spacious home on the Van Beuningenstraat. The house had a large living room and two bedrooms, and an even larger, open basement. This great open space appealed to Ru especially, as it meant she had a place she could use as her studio. Her young life seemed to be filled with promise when disaster struck. The Germans levelled Rotterdam and went on to occupy Holland entirely. Within a few weeks of Holland's surrender, Hitler installed Arthur Seyss-Inquart as *Reichkomissionar*.

The German presence loomed large in the country; in response, the Dutch Resistance crystallized. The lives of Ru and Theodora would never be the same again. Ru felt history was repeating itself. She had been told the story of her own family's persecution countless times, and she was acutely aware of the implications of these drastic changes that were taking place in her country. Her ancestors had been Huguenots who had fled France after the Saint Bartholomew's Day Massacre in 1572. Ru's ancestors had survived because of those that risked their lives to give them refuge, and her family finally found asylum in Holland.

The story of their persecution and escape was transmitted to the descendants of the Huguenots – along with a legacy of compassion toward the victims of discrimination and hatred. Ru was not a religious person but she was a woman of strong conviction, and she respected honesty, integrity, and the performance of good deeds. Her circle of friends consisted of people who came from all walks of life; race, color, or religious creed never entered into her head, but it was clear that all around her, the prevailing mindset of tolerance was being suppressed as the Nazis began their brutal treatment of Jews.

Ru and Theodora decided that they could not be passive in the face of such unthinkable persecution. Ru had friends who were active in the Underground, and she communicated her wish to collaborate with them in any way possible. She organized addresses where Jews could be hidden from the Nazis, and worked on preparing new identity papers for the persecuted. She also raised money tirelessly for any expenses they might incur. She worked intensely within this framework to find new homes for Jewish children within the Catholic and Christian communities – places where they could pass for adopted children, and thus be spared a tragic fate. Ru would deliver the children to their new "underground" homes after connecting them to their new families via the Underground. She and Theodora became the central point of this operation. The moment Ru received a child, she became responsible for his or her safety. She would select and place the child in a home as soon as possible. If she received any indication that the home had become dangerous, for whatever reason, she retrieved the child and found a new safe house for him or her. In order to operate in this way, she relied on trustworthy information from other people, mostly local priests.

Her main contact in Braband was Father Theo Verhoeven, whom she would call when she needed a safe home for her children. Again, she changed her name and adopted the alias of "Tante Zus." Theodora became "Tante Do" after she used her concert proceeds to raise funds for their work. Chris Lebeau, whose numerous illustrations gave his work a recognizable, "official" appearance, prepared all the forged identity papers and cards for their children. They were so well done and legal in their appearance that they easily passed any inspection. Chris was a Christian who was appalled at the atrocities that the Nazis were committing. Together, the three worked to move as many children in danger as possible to safe houses, where they could survive the war.

Efforts to convince Dutch families to shelter Jewish children were also being made throughout the country. Hannah van der Voort came from Tienray, in the Limburg province in the southern Netherlands. Together with Nico Dohmen, she helped find hiding places for 123 Jewish children in the southern Netherlands. Receiving these children through an extensive underground network with which they were affiliated, they sought out and arranged temporary and permanent places of refuge with private families, transferring children from place to place as circumstances warranted. The money for the upkeep by the host families originated with an underground organization. Dohmen, as a courier between the sheltering families and the underground, maintained close contact with the children and devoted much time and effort to counselling his wards and lifting up their spirits. They were given special courses on how to behave as Catholic children, but no one tried to convert them.

Arnold Douwes, the son of a pastor in the Dutch Reformed Church, focused his efforts in the area of Nieuwlande, in the northeast province of Drenthe. Almost every household sheltered Jews in this area, as Arnold and his Jewish friend Max "Nico" Leons, who posed as a Protestant colleague, enlisted the help of several hundred Dutch families in their rescue activities. Another agent, a farmer in Nieuw Vennep (Haarlemeer), southwest of Amsterdam, named Johannes Bogaard, convinced his entire family to help Jews escape the Nazi net. Johannes collected money, ration cards, and identification papers from friends and acquaintances to assist Zus and Father Verhoeven, along with their colleagues, in their work. They were united in their cause to combat the Nazis, and this feeling of solidarity erased any historical grudges or antagonism between the members of the Underground.

Christians of all denominations now united to form one strong resistance. One of Tante Zus's first tasks in 1942 was to help relocate the granddaughter of a Jewish friend. She offered to take the little girl, named Hanna, to a safe home in Ter Apel. Over the next four months, Zus changed Hanna's hideaway at least a dozen times, as she was constantly worried about betrayal by neighbors. These moves were always made unexpectedly. The children would be happy to see her on the one hand, for she always brought something for them, such as a sweater, an orange, or any other delicious treat she could get her hands on, but on the other, they knew that the appearance of Tante Zus meant it was time for them to move again. On one occasion, when she and Hanna were travelling on a train en route to a new hiding place, Hanna asked loudly, "Am I allowed to travel like this, without my star?" The passengers sitting near them were shocked, and Zus and Hanna were forced to get off at the following stop. Zus eventually managed to find a safe home for Hanna, where she remained safe for the rest of the war.

AUTHOR'S NOTE: Tante Zus was honored by Yad Vashem as a Righteous Gentile. A school in Amsterdam was also named in her honor. (Ru Pare Openbare Bassis-school Chris Lebeau straat #4, 1062DC Amsterdam)

LOST IDENTITY

Chapter 8
Arrival at the Labor Camp

Westerbork, April 12, 1943

T HE TRAIN WAS APPROACHING the village of Westerbork in the province of Drente, close to the German border. The Dutch government owned several hundred acres of marshland, and deemed this area to be the ideal location for a refugee camp for the thousands of German Jews who had streamed into Holland after Kristallnacht. Overcome by the number of legal and illegal refugees, the Dutch government had to find a way of providing temporary shelter for the new arrivals. On July 19, 1939, the order was given to start building a camp that would contain barracks, shops, and schools. Caroline remembered the campaign that raised funds for the upkeep of the refugee camp for their fellows Jews. The Committee for Jewish Interests had to bear the cost of more than a million guilders to build the camp with its amenities. Plans were made to accommodate about three thousand people, including facilities to train and prepare the refugees for integration into Dutch society.

The camp was still under construction when the first refugees arrived, and they were recruited to help with the building as well as cultivation of the surroundings. One of the first refugees had complained bitterly to the Jewish community about this overload of work, and Ies was asked to investigate the situation. Caroline recalled how he had described the surroundings: "The further we got, the more desolate it became. At one stage, we could see nothing but uncultivated land with the occasional shrub. This place, reserved for a refugee camp, was nothing more than a vast desolate area."

Caroline stared through the window as the train pulled into Westerbork. It passed slowly through the middle of the camp until it came to a halt at the end of the Boulevard des Miseres, where it began to unload its human cargo. Caroline could see several German officers watching as the *Ordnungsdients* (the Brigade of Jewish Disciplinarians) directed the Jews to the administration office, where they were registered and assigned to their barracks. Caroline got off the train and joined the long line. Her thoughts were far away, focused on the fate of her baby. Suddenly, it was her turn to speak, and she faced the clerk in front of her.

"Name?" he demanded.

"Caroline Kanes," she replied quietly.

"And Levie Kanes…?" he demanded, looking around him, to see if he had overlooked the baby.

"He is still in the hospital in The Hague and will be sent here as soon as the doctors discharge him," Caroline replied.

The clerk looked down on his roster and crossed the name off the list. Beside it, he wrote, "to be sent later," and went back to his work.

The barrack was overwhelming; it was overcrowded with iron beds piled three layers high. Above them hung the drying laundry of hundreds of terrified people. There was no privacy, no space to be had. The hygienic conditions were beneath any standard imaginable. To her exhausted relief, Caroline managed to find a vacant bed. She lay her head down and stretched out, instantly falling asleep. She woke up abruptly. Around her, people were gathering around a man who stood at the entrance to the barrack, calling out names. When he called out the last name on his list, he ordered the "deportees" he had mentioned to prepare for their journey. The women hurriedly organized themselves, causing frenzy and panic to prevail in the barracks. While some women quietly and methodically shoved whatever belongings they owned in their pockets, others cried loudly because their names had been called, while their children were to remain behind. Eighty-three women from Caroline's barrack were ordered to wait with the women from the other barracks. They were led to a train that was waiting for them on the Boulevard des Miseres. Everyone else was told to stay put and await his or her work assignment in the morning.

During all this commotion, Caroline wondered whether she would find Soli. She considered that he might have been shipped off on the transport to the East, like so many of the women in her barracks who had been sent to wait.

"Who are you looking for?" a voice asked.

Caroline tried to identify the person speaking to her. It was the woman who slept in the bunk above hers. She had been watching Caroline from her bunk, who was too preoccupied with her thoughts to notice anyone else around her. She stared at the woman, and said nothing.

"I'm Janie de Hond. I've been here for three weeks. Is there someone here that you know?" she asked. Caroline could see she was not the only one desperately searching the faces around her.

"I am Caroline Kanes. I was looking for my husband, Solomon…Soli." She moved closer to Janie, forcing herself back into the present and out of her search. She sat on her bed and wondered if Janie had, during her time at the camp, come across Soli Kanes. After all, Janie knew everything there was to know about the camp. She told Caroline about the First Lieutenant Albert Konrad Gemmeker, whose main concern was meeting weekly quotas of Jewish deportees. Gemmeker took great pains to be seen as a decent gentleman who treated Jews respectfully. He never interfered with the daily routine of the camp and concentrated solely on that one goal, while maintaining an air of efficiency. He achieved this by delegating the organization of the camp to the prisoners themselves. He offered them what he considered an equitable trade: they would organize and regulate the deportation of prisoners to the labor camps, and in return their own deportation would be delayed. If they were especially productive at meeting the quota, they could expect that their work would save their families, and even their friends, from the fate they were preparing for the deportees.

Gemmeker had created a small elite of German Jews who organized the deportation of Dutch Jews so that the Nazis did not have to directly concern themselves with the task. The chief administrator of the camp, *Oberdienstleider* Kurt Schlessinger, was one of the Jewish elite. His work was considered to be the most important: overseeing the department in which deportation lists were compiled. As long as this department could continue to meet the targeted number of Jewish deportees, it could hold absolute power over the other prisoners in the camp. It was with one of the men in the administrative department that Janie had, herself, struck a bargain. Arthur Pisk, who was the leader of the OD-*Ordnungsdient*, the Service for Preserving Order, had found Janie very attractive, so she was given special privileges that kept her off the transport list.

Caroline was curious what it was exactly that Janie had to do for Arthur Pisk in order to be the beneficiary of such special privileges, which included some very light work in the camp shop. But desperate times called for desperate measures, and nowadays people were willing to do anything, merely to stay alive. Caroline looked at Janie's physical features; she was about the same age as Janie, and had come from the same community. It could just as easily be her who was subject to such "bargains," and wondered what she could do to avoid such a situation. As Caroline was weighing up the various possibilities, the shrill whistling of the departing train sent an abrupt shudder throughout the barracks. Everyone heaved a collective sigh of relief that they had once again eluded the transport.

Janie informed Caroline where she could find the central kitchen and a meal, and Caroline reminded Janie to look for Soli when she went off to work in the camp's shop. They agreed to meet at 2:00 P.M. that afternoon. When the barrack leader asked Caroline to choose between working in the kitchen or in the nursery, Caroline quickly chose the kitchen. It was too painful to think of working with infants; she did not want to be reminded that she had given up her baby.

While standing in line in the kitchen, Caroline suddenly became aware of the people around her. She noticed that some women were wearing nothing more than flimsy pajamas, and many others wore clothes that were wrinkled and tattered. She was still wearing one of her best suits, a birthday gift from Soli, which she had looked forward to wearing after the birth of her child. She finally reached the end of the line, and was given murky soup and two small boiled potatoes, the allotted food for the inmates. It had been a long while since Caroline had eaten. She wondered what would happen to her now. A few minutes before two o'clock, Janie came rushing into the barrack looking for Caroline.

"I've found your husband!" she yelled excitedly. "I've found Soli! He works in the hospital kitchen, sitting and peeling potatoes all day!"

Caroline looked up at her friend in astonishment, not daring to believe that Soli could be so close.

"He works in the hospital kitchen, sitting and peeling potatoes all day!"

Caroline shrieked with joy at the prospect of seeing Soli again.

"How is he? Did you speak to him?" Caroline asked frantically.

"He has had a foot operation and can't walk very well, so they gave him a job that he can do sitting. He finishes work at 5:00 P.M. You can go and see him when he is through." The two women embraced and Caroline counted the minutes until she could finally be reunited with Soli. What was just a few hours seemed like an eternity.

At five, Caroline went in search of Soli, and ran down the hospital corridor to his ward.

"Soli, Soli!" she shouted, uncontrolled in her desire to see her husband again. Upon hearing the familiar voice, Soli turned around to the running figure behind him – he could not believe his eyes.

"Clientje, Clientje!" he shouted, when his voice returned. He hobbled towards Caroline, and as they embraced, each sobbed uncontrollably. It was nothing short of a miracle to find each other after the horror they had both endured. Tears poured down Caroline's face as she held onto Soli with all her strength; it was as if she feared that she would lose him if she let go of him. Soli kissed his beloved wife passionately, and tried to calm the rapid beating of his heart. He told her again and again how much he loved and missed her, and how much he had worried for her and the baby. Caroline felt as if, for the second time, her heart was breaking into tiny pieces when Soli asked about their baby; she did not know how to tell him that their newborn son, Levie, was far away.

Caroline did not wish to break the news in public, so she led Soli out to the evening air, where they could talk in private.

"Soli," she said softly, "I could not bring Levie here with me." She could read in Soli's eyes a potent mixture of fear and sadness. "He was taken by the Resistance, and hopefully placed with a loving family. I did not think there was any other way for him to survive. Hopefully he is in good hands." Soli was unable to find the words to express the torrent of grief and pain that was churning inside him. He found solace in the thought that his precious baby, whom he had never laid eyes on, was safe, protected from the brutal reality his parents were living.

He closed his eyes in a kind of silent prayer for a second, breathed deeply, and then asked, "Where is Ies these days?"

"Ies has left. He made sure that I was looked after in the hospital, and then went on his way. He told me he was going to France to join the Maquis. I have not heard any news of him since he left me at the hospital."

"He has more brains than the rest of us put together," Soli remarked. Caroline and Soli's time together was precious, and Soli wasted no time in sharing his experiences with her since his arrival in Westerbork. One of his friends, a Dutch officer, had informed him of the rumors that Jews were being exterminated as soon as they arrived at the "labor" camps. Those who survived the three-day train ride were killed instantly – and obviously, the infirm, the elderly, and infants were not being used for labor. Soli escaped deportation because of his connection with Dr. Spannier, the Jewish doctor who had been in charge of the hospital since before the war. His operation, which was supposed to correct his flat feet, rendered him officially "unable to travel." Spannier found Soli work in the kitchen, where he could scavenge food for himself, as well as for his parents and cousins, who were also in the camp.

Soli told Caroline that his brother Maurits and his wife Rebecca had been sent to Auschwitz last September along with their two small children. He had no news of them. It was theoretically possible that they were still alive, since there was a labor camp at Auschwitz, but transfer to Sobibor, he had heard, meant certain death.

The Germans were very careful to present Westerbork as a transit camp, and to this end, attempted to make life there appear as normal as possible, providing all sorts of recreational activities for the inmates, including the best cabaret company in Holland, with the best Jewish performers. They introduced sports competitions, with facilities for boxing, soccer, and athletics. All of these facilities, which included a hospital on the camp premises, were designed to create the illusion that the Nazis cared for the Jews in their camps.

Soli described the hospital to Caroline. "It was not just any hospital, it was considered one of the best, in terms of expert medical treatment," he explained. "It was equipped with over 1,700 beds, 120 doctors, and more than 1,000 employees." Soli was aware that the Germans were trying to fool the inmates into thinking that Jews were only being deported in order to contribute to the German war effort. By the end of their stay at Westerbork, they were supposed to be completely healthy. Some inmates had even received letters from relatives who had been sent to Auschwitz, which told of how hard, but bearable, life was there. But Soli feared that Maurits and Rebecca, together with their children, had been murdered. There were no letters from aging parents or from relatives with small children.

Even in the still evening air, Soli and Caroline could not find privacy, so they returned to the hospital, where Soli knew of a place where they could be alone. It would not do for them to talk in the open, as there were too many things to be fearful of. It had also occurred to both of them that they had not been alone together for many months. Soli led Caroline into a storage room with a door he could lock from the inside. Caroline felt renewed hopes that together with Soli, she could survive this ordeal.

Chapter 9
The Golden Lion

THE BELL RANG at Van Beuningenstraat in The Hague, and Tante Do opened the door to Joop Wortman and Father Theo Verhoeven. She led them into the living room, and took the basket, with the baby inside, down to the cellar. There she followed a secret passage that was built behind a soundproof wall. Here Zus had a small office in one corner, consisting of a desk, two chairs, a filing cabinet, and a three-person sofa. On the other side of the room she kept a few cots and a crib for unexpected arrivals.

Zus took the baby from Do and gently placed him in the crib. Zus checked the new arrival and filled in a report with all known details of the baby for the Underground's files. She was surprised to see the red welt on the right side of his tiny body, the sign of a recent operation, and she proceeded to write down her observations.

Zus had revised the latest reports that came in from the Underground agents in the field, supplying her with names of people willing to take in Jewish children, either on a temporary or permanent basis. After surveying the information, Zus went upstairs and invited Father Verhoeven to join her downstairs, where they could discuss their next move, and left Joop and Do chatting over a cup of tea. Zus and Theo acted enigmatically so that if the Germans were to arrest the other two, they could not extract any information out of them.

Zus and Theo settled themselves on the couch, where Zus showed the priest the most recent reports.

"I have an idea," said Theo, after reviewing the information. One of his contacts in Veghel, Tilly Sevriens, had several homes for Jewish children. As a cover, Tilly worked in the Hotel De Gouden Leeuw (the Golden Lion), a hotel and restaurant owned by her cousin Susanne Sevriens Fox and her husband Lambertus Fox. Tilly had told Theo that her cousins would love to adopt a baby boy. Both Zus and Theo agreed that this option seemed the most suitable for this baby, as it was very possible that his parents would not return from the camps.

Father Verhoeven agreed to make the necessary adoption arrangements, while Zus promised to get Chris Lebeau to make an identity card for the baby and herself, in case of a German inspection. The priest went upstairs and quickly departed with Joop.

Later that afternoon, Zus received a call, asking her to deliver her "painting" the following day to the Golden Lion in Veghel – they had reserved for her a first-class seat on the train. Father Verhoeven was also booked on the same coach, headed for his parish in Veghel. In this way, he could keep an eye on Zus. That evening, Zus received the necessary identity cards for her trip in the morning to Veghel.

Zus boarded the train from the Central Station in The Hague at 6:45 A.M. She was now Maria Schouten. She and her little baby, Piet, were travelling back home to Veghel after visiting her family in The Hague. As Zus entered the coach, she spotted six seats, three of them occupied on one side by two Dutch policemen and a priest. Zus sat across from the priest.

"Good morning Father," she greeted the priest.

"Good morning to you, my child," he replied.

She then saluted the policemen, "Good morning gentlemen," and they both responded in tandem, "Good morning madam."

At this early hour, Zus was a sight for sore eyes; she was a tall, slim elegant woman in her mid-forties, who very much looked the part of an aristocratic society woman, in her stylish brown slacks and beautiful yellow satin blouse. Her high-heeled brown leather shoes gave her outfit an added edge. Zus had dressed the baby in a cute little suit that she had stored for these occasions. Just as the train whistle blew, another well-dressed gentleman entered the cabin and sat next to Zus. He took out the local newspaper from the inside of his coat and started to read. Zus felt a slight tremor of fear, a sort of sixth sense, that this man might be a Nazi collaborator. A glance at Father Verhoeven told her that he harbored the same suspicions. The train passed Utrecht, and the two policemen got off. The man next to Zus remained in the coach with them.

The priest ventured to make small talk with Maria. "And where would you be headed for with this lovely baby?" he inquired.

"Oh, I am just going home to my family in Veghel. I spent a few days in The Hague with my cousin who was dying to see my son," she replied.

It was almost nine o'clock when the train reached Hertogenbosch, and Zus and Father Verhoeven descended from the train. They both felt instant relief when the suspicious-looking man continued on to Eindhoven.

They briskly walked over to the main bus station, where at 9:30 they boarded the 158 line, which read *Hertogenbosch–Rosmalen–Berlicum–Middelrode–Heeswijk–Veghel*. They arrived at the Veghel station at 10:45, where Tilly Sevriens was waiting for them. Father Verhoeven introduced Zus to Tilly, and they walked the short block from the bus station to the Golden Lion Hotel. Tilly led the way to the first floor, where the Fox family lived. Their arrival caused quite a stir. Susanne Fox, a good-looking, robust woman of thirty-nine years, and Lambertus "Bertie" Fox, her thirty-four-year-old husband, were anxiously awaiting the arrival of their little baby boy. Their three-year-old daughter, Lia, was all spruced up for the occasion.

Father Verhoeven introduced the Foxes to Zus Pare. Once the formalities were over, Susanne wasted no time in picking up her new son. "Oh my, what a beautiful little baby!" she exclaimed.

Bertie had wanted a son for so long, but since she could no longer have children, they had decided to adopt.

Father Verhoeven, Zus, and Tilly stayed for lunch, and discussed the local situation. Tilly told them about Father Lodewijk Bleijs, the priest in charge of resistance activities in the Nijmegen district. At the beginning of the year, he had initiated a major effort to offer safe hiding places to Jews or escaped prisoners of war.

The consensus of opinion amongst them was that the tide was turning, and that it was only a matter of time before the Germans would be defeated.

Zus and Theo thanked their hosts, and Zus returned to the bus station, while the priest headed for the Veghel parish, where he would meet with Father Bleijs later on.

Chapter 10
Westerbork: A Living Hell

May 1943

CAROLINE FEARED her character was changing with each day she spent at Westerbork. She became hardened to the world around her, and her senses had become blunted. The suffering she witnessed from week to week was more than she could comprehend. She didn't want to think or feel anymore – the pain was too intense to handle. The barracks were enough to destroy any human's spirit. They were saturated with mud and surrounded by barbed wire. Caroline noticed the scratched faces of children who accidentally ran into, or fell against, the barbed wire in their attempts at play and sometimes, escape.

There were shortages of all different kinds in the camp, but the worst shortage by far was the severe lack of space. The misery was palpable. People were forced into tiny, cramped spaces, three to a bed, one bed piled on top of another, stacked alongside the prisoners' meager belongings. At night many prisoners would lie awake, unable to sleep either because of the loud cries of the children, or simply because they were so cramped that they couldn't find a comfortable position to sleep in. Wet laundry festooned the barracks. The moans of the sick and ailing children penetrated even those hanging clothes, so that the sound of suffering pervaded every corner of the barracks.

The plague of flies was unbearable; as if aware of the squalor and misery, the flies gravitated towards the mud and swamps of the barracks. As a result, most people suffered from eye infections. The water was practically undrinkable, contributing to the prevailing sickness throughout the barracks. The misery was indescribable. The conditions were so hideous that Caroline wondered at how anyone managed to retain their sanity. She felt like a rat living in a sewer; such humiliation should surely induce human beings to take their own lives. She marvelled at the human endurance and courage displayed at Westerbork.

Soli helped Caroline to transfer from the central kitchen to the hospital, where she worked as an orderly, and they were assigned to Barracks 66 as a married couple. In the hospital, Caroline looked after the most infirm of the elderly patients. She did not relish her work at the hospital, and could not stop thinking about her little baby, Levie, but at least Soli was nearby. That meant the world to her. She also thought about the many trainloads of prisoners arriving from Amersfoort, with haunted expressions on their freshly bruised faces. When there were not enough prisoners to make up the quota, Schlessinger would select camp inmates to be shipped out with them. One day, Caroline had watched him dispense of two hundred patients in her own ward. It was an excruciating nightmare, one from which she never woke up, to have to help the Nazis by preparing helpless invalids for deportation.

Caroline hurried through the crowd of prisoners who had just arrived, and helped as many as she could find their meager belongings. Her superior was impatient with the amount of time this took, and ordered Caroline to wheel out on stretchers the patients who were about to be deported towards the waiting train. Although she curbed her emotions by being active, she could not fully suppress the intense anger that was burning inside her, as she attempted to calm one woman who was about to be pushed onto the train. The patient, a petite and delicate grandmother of eighty-three, asked her, "Do you think that the medical facilities are as good in Poland as they are here?"

Caroline could not find the words to tell this sweet, unassuming woman what really awaited her at the end of the deadly train journey. Lieutenant Gemmeker ordered Caroline to hurry as she pushed yet another stretcher. Seventy-five people had been loaded into the car, and Caroline could see it was already overcrowded. Very few provisions had been made for comfort or need; there was a bucket placed at the side of the car, which was to be used as a toilet, and a bag of sand, so that each person could cover his or her bodily waste with a handful of it. There was also a small supply of water for consumption in another corner, and paper mattresses were spread out on the floor for the sick.

She witnessed hundreds of people being shoved onto the train: young, old, crippled, sick, demented, or blind. Once in the train, they found themselves squashed up against each other, in between odd pieces of baggage. Any sign of hesitation or slowness was rewarded with brutal kicks; some were even tossed into the cattle cars. What disturbed Caroline most, though, was the amount of Jews who chose to work alongside the Nazis. Standing just a few feet away, Caroline saw the camp's commandant, Lieutenant Gemmeker, with his Jewish secretary, who was sharply dressed in riding breeches and a chestnut-brown jacket. His ostentatious dress and his powerful and arrogant demeanor stood in grotesque contrast to the wasted, devastated expressions on the faces of the inmates. They were joined by Schlessinger, the *Oberdienstleider*, who had the final say in which of the inmates would be spared and which would be shipped out. He walked with an intimidating confidence, dressed in a black army topcoat, black boots, and a cap. With his cruelly set mouth and powerful neck, he could have passed for any SS officer, but his yellow star gave him away. He was a Jew, just like the other unfortunates, yet different from the rest of them, because he could play God in deciding who would live and who would die.

The orderlies who herded everyone onto the overcrowded trains were actually, Caroline noticed, the hated "Jewish SS," German and Dutch Jews who were eager to use their ignorant, brute strength against their own people, in exchange for their petty demands. They dressed in Nazi garb, in green uniforms and high boots. The prisoners hated these traitors with a passion. It was common knowledge that the Jewish SS were supplied with cheap cigarettes and prostitutes in exchange for their efforts. The Jewish SS wasted no opportunity to flaunt their prizes to all those they dominated. Caroline considered them no worse than the agents of Lippman, Rosenthal & Company, the Jewish-owned bank hired by the Germans to reclaim the assets still held by their Jewish clientele. Although the Jewish employees of the bank were forced to cooperate with the Germans, they displayed uncompassionate behavior towards their fellow Jews.

The Jewish accomplices hounded the deportees like beggars, extracting any possessions that had not been entrusted to the care of their friends and family. Like vampires, who suck the blood from their victims while they are still alive, the agents fought over small bank notes, watches, jewels, and anything else thought to be of value. The spectacle sent shivers down Caroline's spine, as she suddenly felt a thick cloud of death engulfing her surroundings. She knew that if she wanted to survive the experience, she would somehow have to desensitize herself to the horrors in the camp. Finally the doors of the train shut. The commandant rode his bicycle down the length of the train, checking all the cars as he went, and, declaring the train to be fully secure, passed his bicycle to his secretary before waving the train on. Caroline waited for the whistle; when it pierced the air with its shriek, another 1,600 Jews were deported from Holland, never to return.

The stream of helpers returned to their quarters, some heartbroken at witnessing the agony of their fellow Jews, but most were numb, as if in a daze. This was not the first time they had witnessed the weekly transport, and they were becoming immune to its effects. Caroline was shocked back into reality – it was a bad enough scenario that the inmates were being sent to work in labor camps, but she could not stomach the truth that the elderly, babies, and the sick were being sent to their deaths. Caroline found solace and the strength to continue living at the thought of her baby Levie, whom she still hoped to find one day. Soli had done his best to be Caroline's confidant, absorbing all her experiences, worries and sorrow. He listened carefully as Caroline would describe her day, and noted the growing sound of defeat in her words. Each person at the camp thought constantly about his or her own hopelessness and fear; it disturbed him to think that Caroline might begin to fall prey to those fears.

"Clientje," he said, softly, "why don't we cheer ourselves up by going to visit the family?" He was hoping his light tone would lift her spirits a little. "We could see how they are doing. They'll tell us stories and take our minds off today." Caroline sighed deeply and looked into her husband's warm, comforting eyes.

"Of course," she said, "you always know what will make me feel better."

They walked across the camp after six o'clock, passing one of the watchtowers on the way. In the field beyond the fence lay a thick blanket of purple blooms. Lupines perfumed the air just outside the camp, and the breeze-tossed flowers were like a balm to Caroline.

"Wait here, Clientje," whispered Soli, as he walked toward the barbed wire fence and the flowers. There was a small gap under the fence, just large enough to accommodate his hand and arm as they stretched toward the pink and blue flower stalks. Soli gathered a bouquet together and handed the flowers to Caroline.

"Here, Clientje," he said, smiling, "Now, we will not arrive empty-handed." Soli's cousins Jansje and Mozes Lootsteen lived in a wooden hut with their five children. They lived not far from Caroline and Soli's barracks, and were assigned to a hut that was allotted for large families. The hut was tiny and sparsely furnished, but even so, it was a haven compared to the crowded and harsh conditions of the barracks. Jansje stood at the stove in the middle of the kitchen, busily preparing a cabbage stew. When Jansje saw her cousins at the door, she immediately stopped what she was doing, and ran to kiss Caroline and Soli, graciously accepting their gift of flowers.

"Come in, come in," she said, ushering them into the warm area by the stove where she worked. "Mozes should be back soon – when he returns, you will join us for dinner. How sweet of you to bring flowers!"

Caroline looked around the small, light, space. It was good to see her cousin, even though she knew life was very hard for them too. Jansje was equally as happy to see them. Mozes arrived home with Soli's cousins, Abraham and Rebecca Kanes, and their daughter Lea. Everyone crowded in together, warmer for each other's company despite the scarcity of space. Besides the tiny kitchen that also served as a dining area, there were two more small rooms and a washroom in the hut. All seven of the Lootsteens, as well as the three Kaneses, lived in these small allotments together. The hut was furnished with nothing more than the rudimentary fixtures. There was a faucet and workstand in the area where Jansje stood, a table and some chairs, but little else. As cramped as they were, Caroline envied them. Here at least, away from the barracks, they could openly share their feelings, and luxuriate in the knowledge that they were talking in privacy.

The adults, who sat on chairs, and the children who sat on the cold floor, were fed a bowl of hot cabbage soup; it was watery, but satisfying enough for a group of people who were perpetually hungry. The adults let the children eat first, as there were not enough bowls and utensils to go around. When they finished, they were sent off to bed with little resistance. Once the last toddler had been put to bed, all the adults gathered around the table for their own meal and conversation.

Jansje did what she could with the cabbage she was given, always a small amount to work with, given the number of mouths that needed feeding and the amount of work they were expected to do. The adults would smuggle vegetables from the fields, which were guarded by the Marechaussee; the former Dutch police officers would never begrudge them extra food. When Jansje was lucky enough to have extra vegetables to work with, she managed to rustle up a tasty meal. Caroline gulped down the soup greedily; this was the most substantial meal than she had eaten in months.

Abraham and Mozes were thin and sunburned from their work in the fields, but they were still vibrant and healthy. The Nazis preferred family men to work in their gardens, since they felt they were less likely to attempt escape if their families accompanied them to the camps. Abraham and Mozes felt their productivity was an assurance against their demise – if they continued to work hard, they would evade deportation. It was everyone's worst fear that families and friends would be forced to separate, shipped out by transport to different labor, or even worse, extermination camps.

The group talked about their family, lamenting the death of their Aunt Lea Kanes Zwalf. Lea had raised sixteen children (Abraham and Jansje were her son and daughter) and had worked hard all her life. She had been put on a transport only a few days before, while her husband Barent had been sent to Auschwitz several months earlier. Lea would surely be murdered in the new camp, they assumed. She was sixty-eight years old and was no longer able to meet the Nazis' criteria for healthy workers. Since her husband was shipped to Auschwitz months before, Lea had lost her will to continue. She knew that death awaited him there, and it was only a matter of time before she would join him.

Jansje cried when she spoke to Soli about his own mother and father. Only two weeks earlier, Levie and Esther had been put on the train to Sobibor. Jansje told them how she and Mozes had been given the opportunity to prepare suitcases for their journey to Westerbork; a Dutch policeman had come to their house to instruct them to present themselves at the Schouwberg the following day, bringing along one suitcase per person, packed with the necessary clothes and blankets. Schouwberg was a famous theater in Amsterdam that was converted, during wartime, to a central meeting point from where the Jews were deported to Westerbork.

Soli's parents, and others like them, were not as lucky. They had been rounded up in sudden raids, and were only permitted to take with them their slippers, underwear, and pajamas – only the clothes on their backs. Caroline had come across many of these victims at the camp, recent arrivals who had been dragged out of their homes in the middle of the night. She was amazed at how they survived the train journey in such flimsy clothing – it was a miracle that they managed to endure the freezing conditions.

Escape was a subject that was constantly being discussed in the camp, but the Nazis had devised several deterrents, and recent events had quieted this notion. There had been an all-out search for an escaped prisoner, a member of the group that had been transported that week from the Vught detention camp. Under the supervision of the SS troops, who were specially trained to "deal" with Jews, the men had laid the railway tracks from Hooghaalen to the camp. However in Westerbork, daily supervision was in the hands of the Marechaussee, who were generally good-hearted, mild men.

Upon arriving at Westerbork, the men from Vught learned that their families had been shipped out the day before. They were furious. The Germans had promised that as a reward for their hard labor they would be reunited with their families, and the betrayal was a terrible blow. This prompted one slave laborer to escape. The escape itself was successful, but the Germans meted out collective punishments for such incidents. This time, the whole camp had to stand outside in the pouring rain until the escaped prisoner was returned. No food or water was given to the prisoners, and many of the elderly collapsed and were left lying in the mud. The prisoner was not caught, and as a result, forty people were selected for deportation on the next train. As usual, torturous punishments were inflicted on the remaining prisoners. This was often the case until escapees were found or killed. In this way, the Nazis discouraged any escape attempts in their lightly guarded enclaves. Anyone who entertained thoughts of escape had only suicide as recourse to imprisonment; the price of their freedom was too great.

At first glance, Westerbork appeared to be attractive, with its several amenities offered by the Nazis, but the prisoners were soon jolted out of their false sense of security. The gleaming hospitals and schoolrooms were certainly meant to give a positive impression of the wonderful care available to the sick and elderly, but this illusion was quickly shattered when the patients were the first to be shipped to the death camps. Why would the Nazis go to such lengths to create a good impression of the camp, the prisoners wondered. No one knew the answer. All they could hope for was that the war would soon come to an end, as the Nazis were clearly losing ground.

Caroline and Soli left their cousins with the hope that the end to the war would come soon. They had no idea at the time, but they would never see their cousins again. They were all shipped to Sobibor in the following summer months. Unrest grew, intensifying within the camp during that long, hot summer.

The Dutch began to take steps against the Nazi camps they were forced to live beside. It was rumored that the mayor of Belen had been shot in one such uprising, and was brought to the Westerbork camp for interrogation and revenge. In the neighboring fields of Drente, the Dutch burned huge fires of protest against the German occupation.

Caroline and Soli would gather with other prisoners to air their grievances. The veterans of the camp, basically anyone who had lasted more than two months, knew their way around the grounds. Although from the outside, all the barracks looked alike, and were each furnished in the same austere style, there were great differences between them. In some, prisoners felt that they were in the slums, while in others they felt as if they were located in a middle-class district. Each barrack radiated its own atmosphere. Thus, the prisoners favored certain barracks for their meetings, one in particular with a Bohemian corner where the inmates would light candles and discuss history and philosophy.

They listened as Vas Nunes, a worker of the Jewish Council, traced the origin of the animosity between Dutch and German Jews; the tension between the two nationalities in the camp was starting to get out of hand. The resentment between the two groups was fuelled when the first of the German refugees, who had hoped to settle in Amsterdam, were imprisoned in the camp. They had grown bitter and disillusioned when the Dutch Jews showed indifference to their plight. When the Dutch Jews arrived in 1942, along with members of their Jewish Council, the camp was already being managed by German Jews, under the leadership of Kurt Schlessinger, who became the *Oberdienstleider*. The Jewish Council quickly discovered that Schlessinger was the only person to whom they could turn regarding all camp issues. Unfortunately, he had little respect for the council. Schlessinger delegated some roles to Dutch Jews, such positions as doctors in the hospital, or barrack leaders. He reserved the key functions for the German Jews, in order to assure their privileged selection practices. From the very first transport of Jews to the East, the German Jews filled the weekly quotas with Dutch Jews, healthy or sick, in order to delay putting their own on the trains. The German Jews also had a dangerous habit of behaving maliciously against their Dutch counterparts. They screamed and barked just like Prussian sergeants. The Dutch Jews resented and hated the arrogance of these German Jews. As the German defeat seemed to be on the horizon, many of the German Jews began to fear that after the war, the Dutch Jews would retaliate against them.

Vas Nunes explained that there was a slight improvement in Schlessinger's attitude towards the Dutch inmates, as more German Jews found themselves on the transport list. These discussions injected new hope into the despondent inmates. The evenings would come to a close with the group quietly singing *Ani Ma'amin*, the Hebrew affirmation of belief in the coming of the Messiah.

On Friday, September 10, 1943, Caroline and Soli ate dinner together in the hospital canteen. Caroline said, "Ach, Soli, I miss Shabbat evening dinner at my parent's home." She remembered nostalgically how her mother, Henriette, would always make the Shabbat special so that each of the seven children would know the difference between weekday and Shabbat. Her parents always dressed in their finest attire, and clothed their children in fresh, clean dresses and suits. They would sit around the beautifully decorated table, enjoying the items that Henriette had bought with money that she had saved.

Henriette Haag had grown up in a very religious Jewish home. She took it upon herself to ensure that her children received a good Jewish education, and had struggled to make sure that Caroline and her siblings could attend Sunday *cheder* school, where they would be instructed in the Jewish customs and laws. Caroline fantasized that she was eating delicious *peeren koegel* and *challes* (pear cake and braided bread) that her mother used to make, and with every bite of her own meager food, she savored the sweet memories. She was grateful that her mother had died peacefully, and been buried with dignity in Toepat, the Rotterdam Jewish cemetery.

She had been spared the horror that other family members were forced to endure with the war. Caroline regretted, however, that her father had not been so lucky. He had been killed at Auschwitz just months before.

On Monday night, September 13, Caroline and Soli learned that they were to leave for Auschwitz the following morning. Caroline celebrated her thirty-third birthday on a train that was headed East.

Chapter 11
Hiding in Veghel

April 14, 1943

W HEN THE BABY BOY, Levie Kanes, was brought to their home, Susanne and Bertie Fox renamed him Johannes, and nicknamed him Jantje, because they were so in love with him. They were so overjoyed to finally have a precious little baby boy, and were even more delighted when Lia, his new older sister, demonstrated how much she loved her new baby brother. This was a memorable day for the Fox family. For months, Susanne and Bertie were terrified at the prospect of being caught harboring a Jewish child, but as soon as they laid eyes on their new son, all their fear dissipated. Despite the war and ongoing turmoil, Susanne and Bertie began to feel renewed optimism about the future. Susanne hadn't felt so happy in a long time; the baby gave her a sense of fulfillment, helping her to forget, albeit only for short intervals, the difficult times they were living in.

As Susanne prepared Jan for his bath for the first time, she reflected on how many wonderful changes had come about because of this new welcome addition to their family. She had converted Lia's bedroom into a room with a nursery, brightly decorated with colorful curtains and bed linen, cheery lamps, and an abundance of baby toys. For weeks she had saved money so that she could buy new clothing for her son. Now that Jan

83

was finally here, and was no longer the object of a dream, he delighted the entire house with the sound of his voice.

Susanne carefully selected a warm, light-blue outfit from the assortment of clothes she had purchased, then placed the clothing out on the bed while the water ran for his bath. Once in the bath, Jantje squealed with delight and splashed vigorously with his little feet. He was simply gorgeous with his curls and big hazel eyes.

As she bathed him, Susanne noticed his circumcision, and was awakened to how dangerous it was to harbor a Jewish child. She shuddered at the thought of the Nazis searching her baby for the marks of this procedure, but then banished the nightmarish image from her mind. She hoped the false papers Tante Zus had provided would satisfy any potential inspection.

Several days later, Jantje developed blisters and a high fever. Susanne quickly wrapped Jantje in a blanket and ran to Dr. Kerkhof. The kind doctor had treated her family for years, and Susanne did not fear his reaction to the baby, but she discovered that her trust had been misplaced; she could not possibly have predicted such a hostile attitude when the doctor saw the circumcision.

"What do you mean by bringing this child here?" he demanded, noting Jan's scars. "Don't you know that it is forbidden for me to treat Jews? Leave with your baby at once!"

Susanne had never seen the doctor so angry before. She bundled up her son, and made one last attempt to appeal to the doctor's better nature. "He will die if you don't help him, Doctor. His fever is so high!"

But Dr. Kerkhof remained stone-hearted as he listened to her wailing.

"I can't help you," he insisted. "The Nazis will shoot me if they find out he's even been here!"

Susanne stared wordlessly at the man she thought she had known all her life.

"Now," he shouted, "get out before I report you!"

Susanne glared at the doctor and stormed out of the office. She was speechless with fury and was terrified that the baby would die before anyone could treat him. Tilly saw her run into the hotel with the bundle in her arms, and held the baby while Susanne went in search of her husband. Just then, Bertie came in and noticed his wife's distress.

"What happened?" he asked, concerned about Jan's well-being.

"Dr. Kerkhof will not help us," said Susanne, curbing the anger in her voice.

Bertie ran off into another room. Susanne heard him loudly turning the room upside down until he found what he was looking for. Bertie emerged with a pistol and began to wrap up the baby for yet another journey to the doctor's house.

"I'll show that bastard," he yelled as he ran outdoors.

Kerkhof was shocked to find Bertie at his door, with the baby in one arm and a loaded pistol in the other. His voice was deep and quiet, as he spoke to the doctor, saying, "You won't have to worry about the Nazis shooting you. If you don't treat my son immediately, I'll shoot you myself!" Bertie announced, shocked at his own determination.

The doctor turned pale, then straightened his stance, and took the bundled child from Bertie's arm. He put the baby down on the examining table, unwrapped his diaper, and then gathered his instruments. Silently, Bertie kept watch as the doctor worked. When the doctor finished writing out his script, and a set of clear instructions for Jantje, he silently turned away, in the hope that Bertie would leave quietly. Bertie slammed his money on the doctor's desk and whispered, "You'd better keep this quiet, or I'll make sure we will both pay the penalty." He gathered up his child and left for home.

As the Foxes adjusted to life with their new son, Father Verhoeven, Tilly, and the Hoogenhoffs continued to take in Jews who desperately needed safe homes. Some of their imperilled charges did not end well. The Tilaart family in Zeitart was just one example of the failure of well-laid plans. The family, consisting of a couple with eleven children, were always eager to help anyone in distress, and readily worked with the Hoogenhoffs to house anyone in need.

Bertha van de Tilaart, one of the daughters, took in a Jewish woman with false identity papers, named Fientje Huis. She was thirty-eight and originally from Scheveningen. When the Nazis "cleaned up" the houses in their area, Fientje had been forced to move from place to place in order to remain hidden. Unfortunately, she had just undergone a kidney operation, and was in dire need of a safe place where she could recuperate. She moved in with the Tilaart family and established contact with the Rector van Delft in the local parish. She was preparing to convert to Christianity, and her contact with the rector enabled her to study and to prepare for this change. She made other changes too. She adjusted her appearance in order to blend in with the Tilaart family as much as possible. With her bleached hair, impending conversion, and false identity papers, she began to feel safe in her hiding place. But all that was about to change.

Gestapo officers arrived at the Tilaart farm to arrest the woman who called herself Fientje. Bertha van de Tilaart later described the following regarding Fientje's fate:

"Returning from Veghel, I was warned by my neighbor that there was a 'control' action going on at our farm," she explained. "Well, this had happened before, so I bicycled into our yard, not suspecting anything out of the ordinary. I entered the rear door and three men flew at me and asked my mother, 'Is this she?' 'No,' my mother had replied, 'this is my daughter.' My mother had to point me out on a family portrait in order to convince them. With my dark complexion, I could easily have resembled a Jew. We were ordered to cease our work and gathered in the living room, where we were told to stay put. I asked permission to go up to my room so that I could warn Fientje to stay away, in the event that she arrived too soon. This took too long and I was ordered to come back downstairs. With shaky knees, I impatiently waited to see what would happen. The Nazis met Fientje at the back door and roughly pushed her inside, snatched the purse she was carrying from her hands, and emptied its contents onto the living room table, when a rosary fell out. One of the three officers grabbed the rosary and tossed it across the room violently.

"'*Das ist camouflage; das haben sie allen.*' They knew that her name was not really Fientje, but Mrs. Goldstein from Amsterdam, who had once practiced law in Amsterdam's juvenile court. She was the mother of two children whom she had left behind, Anne Marie and Maurice. The Nazis took her with them and that is the last we saw of her. About a week later we received a short note from her, via the Resistance, which read, 'Thanks for everything, Fientje.' It was her last message from Amersfoort. After that, she was taken to Dachau where she was murdered."

As a result of the tragic incident with Fientje, the underground group came up with a new idea. All Jews would receive several lessons in Protestantism. The group did not dare to pass the refugees off as Catholics, as the farmers would soon uncover the lie, but Protestantism, on the other hand, could be learned. Thus, they were taught the Protestant "Our Father" and the commencement of Christianity. As a result of the refugees posing as Protestants, there were far more families willing to help these people. Theo Verhoeven would plead, "The man or woman is not Catholic, but they are Christians, and it is our duty to help Protestants as well."

Arnold, Paula, and Theo were adamant that should a "converted" Jew be caught, the people sheltering them could at least maintain that they did not know that they were harboring a Jew, thus minimizing the risk to themselves and their families. Several months after the drama with Fientje, Bertha was approached by the courier, Gre van Dijk, to find a home for a one-and-a-half-year-old girl. Bertha was at a loss who to turn to, since the people in the village who were willing to help were already hosting refugees. Bertha received permission from her family to bring the child home.

Courier Gre van Dijk handed the little girl over to Bertha, who put her in a small basket attached to the back of her bike, and pedalled home. "I told the neighbors that she was an orphan from the Rotterdam bombing, and strangers that she was my daughter," she explained. "She was a very sweet child whose real name was Selma de Windt, but we called her Irma. Soon after Irma arrived, another *onderduiker* from Amsterdam, called Bert Meyer, turned up. He stayed with us until after the war. We then harbored a girl called Stientje Keizer, followed by Alie Heemskerk, both from Amsterdam. Constant tension and the fear of being discovered prevailed on the Hoeve Corsica. The *onderduikers* in the area would frequently visit us in the evenings to listen to 'Radio Oranje.' Since this radio was hidden in the attic, at the top of the staircase, there were often ten of us lying on the stairway to listen to the latest news. There were also several Jews in hiding in Uden who received ration cards from the organization. The Hoogenhoffs were involved in handing out ration cards for quite a while, but they became scared that something might go wrong, so I continued with this task. You can imagine the fear I felt after the Fientje affair."

One always had to be on guard. One morning, at about five o'clock, there was a loud knock on Bertha's front door. She woke up immediately, looked out the window, and saw five soldiers. Quickly, she grabbed Irma out of her bed and stuffed her under the blankets in her sister's bed. The Nazis had come to fetch Bertha's brother, Piet, for labor in Germany. Luckily, he had official documents that allowed him to remain at home so that he could attend to the farm. When they were satisfied with the authenticity of the document, they left. Bert Meyer, the *onderduiker,* also slept through this episode at the back of the house.

A few days later, Tilly Sevriens had the scare of her life. She was reading in a room on the second floor of the Golden Lion Hotel, where she would look after Jan while Susanne was busy attending to the clients. Jantje was playing in a playpen, and on a bed in the corner lay a young Jewess called Mona Cohen from Amsterdam, whom Tilly had brought home temporarily until Theo Verhoeven could place her in a safe house.

There was a sudden harsh knock on the door. She barely managed to reach the door when the knocking became even louder and more persistent. She opened the door to find two SS officers standing in front of her. Mustering up all her courage, she confronted them, *"Was willen sie hier?"* she boldly shouted at them, expressing her annoyance at being disturbed.

"Oh sorry, wrong room," they replied and continued down the hall. Tilly closed the door, and nearly fell to the ground, as she tried to regain her composure and breath. She could hear her heartbeat hammering away in her chest, and it took her a while before she could breathe normally again. Upon seeing little Jantje chuckling in the playpen, and Mona sleeping peacefully in the corner, Tilly kneeled down and thanked Jesus for the compassion he had showed her.

"Jan" and his neighbor in Veghel, 1944

"Jan" with Susanne Fox (center) and Aunt Tilly (right), 1944
Woman on left, Toby, worked at the hotel

Chapter 12
Auschwitz

CAROLINE AND SOLI were pushed forward in the long, crowded line as it surged towards the train on the platform. They tried to stay together in the crush, carrying a few pieces of clothing each, and a few provisions that they had managed to rustle up in preparation for the trip. The couple were paralyzed with confusion, fear, and sorrow. Many in the line were infirm, excellent targets for the guards to prod and kick. It was 11:00 A.M. when the doors to the wagon were closed behind them, and they found themselves locked in the car. The shrill sound of the departure whistle indicated that they would begin to move at any moment.

The wagon was crowded and filthy, like every other Caroline had seen come and go since her arrival at the camp. There were about eighty prisoners ensconced within the tiny, enclosed space. At least half of them were either elderly and sick, or far too young to realize what was going on around them. There was no fresh water and very few provisions for their basic needs.

Caroline stared silently around her. She had grown numb as she walked into the cattle car, and now could only huddle against Soli. She had not eaten in several days, and was covered in her own sweat and dirt. Soli was her only comfort as he stayed close by – she kept reminding herself that she was not alone, and unlike many other unfortunate women, did not have to worry about her husband's whereabouts or health. But this was a small consolation when faced with the uncertain prospect of what awaited them in Poland. She thought about her old life – once upon a time, she had been tall, strong, and robust, and now look at her. She and Soli were just human rubble. The trip was easier to deal with, and the thoughts less horrifying, if she and Soli could keep themselves busy by helping other prisoners. They shared their little packet of food with some children who were whimpering from hunger, and they endeavored to make some of the sick passengers more comfortable.

The train car was just a deep, black room consisting of wooden slats roughly nailed to a frame: it had many gaps in the walls that let drafts of freezing cold air seep through. Even with the heat of the thick mass of bodies, the cold was unforgiving. Through the openings, Caroline could see the passing green streaks as the train moved through the countryside and forest toward Poland. When she saw the word "Cracow" on a sign through one of these gaps in the wooden planks, she knew they had arrived in Poland. It was Friday morning when she had seen the sign rush by. By evening they had reached the Auschwitz-Birkenau camp. They had survived four days without water, food, fresh air, or a latrine. They knew what lay ahead could only be more fearful.

The doors of their car were violently thrown open by officers carrying machine guns. The cement platform was crowded with SS officers dragging the prisoners impatiently out of the wagon. "*Raus, Raus*! [Out, out!]"; "*Alles liegen lassen!* [Leave everything!]," they barked. After being suffocated for so long on the crowded train, Caroline and Soli found it difficult to move. They hurried out of the doors, clambering over the bodies of those who did not survive the journey. As they passed they were pummelled with cudgels. They all filed quickly past the frenzied German shepherd dogs, who were barely restrained by the guards. Confusion abounded as orders were screamed out, dogs barked, and huge search lights glared around them in the enclosed camp. The air was contaminated with thick, acrid smoke from the crematoria, and the smell of burning flesh permeated the air.

Caroline lost Soli in the crowd immediately. She watched as he was led away from her with a long line of men across the camp. She was pushed into a line of her own, and was directed by SS guards to the head of a cattle ramp. There they stood and waited until an SS officer decided their next move. Caroline observed the officer, and noted that he looked out of place in the confusion; his countenance was serene, even though agony and death surrounded him. He was very handsome and smiled faintly to himself while he worked. He held himself proudly in his impeccable black uniform. When she looked closely to discern his rank, she noticed his breast pocket decorated with regal embroidery. It bore the medical caduceus. He cheerfully whistled "Liebenstraum," an opera tune, while he searched the women implacably. With the assistance of a riding crop, he directed each inmate to her destination, either to the left or right. Caroline could not have known, but he was indulging himself in his favorite activity: he delighted in selecting which of the new arrivals were fit to work and which would be sent to their deaths.

Caroline was sent to the left. Older women and women with children were directed to the right, then loaded onto trucks and carried away. Caroline breathed a shallow sigh of relief that she and others were chosen to work – which meant survival – for now. Wordlessly, the officer left the women selected to work with a group of SS guards. Having completed his task at hand, he arrogantly walked towards his living quarters. This was Caroline's first encounter with the infamous Dr. Josef Mengele, but it would not be her last.

At this point, Caroline and the others were taken to be shaved and deloused. Her clothes and personal belongings were unceremoniously taken away by the expressionless veterans of the camp, who had hardened themselves to life at the camp. They were so robotic in their actions that they hardly seemed human at all. A skeleton in a striped jacket shaved her head, underarms, and pubis without making a sound or changing his expression. After this first ordeal was over, Caroline joined the others, and waited for hours in the freezing cold, burning just enough strength to shiver. While many of the women collapsed from humiliation and exhaustion, Caroline focused all her thoughts on her son, Levie. Whatever she was going through now, at least she knew that her son was warmly clothed and sleeping peacefully in a soft crib. She rejoiced that he was now with a family who she imagined adored him, and these thoughts sustained her during unbearable conditions. During the delousing, and the freezing showers afterward, she envisioned the snug and warm home in the country where her baby surely lived. When she was handed a threadbare striped cotton dress that was at least two sizes too small for her, she imagined her son wrapped in warm clothing or wearing stylish new outfits. But eventually she was snapped out of her reverie. She was grateful to be able to cover her body, even if it was sorely inadequate.

All around her, the prisoners were being examined again. This time, dental instruments were being thrust into their mouths as new fingers sought out gold fillings. As the fillings were being extracted from the petrified women, she braced herself for the sudden screams of the victims. She was ashamed that she was spared such pain, when there were no fillings to be found. Finally, she was tattooed with a number six digits long: her new identity was 312658. The assignment of numbers was just one of the Nazis' methods of dehumanizing their prisoners, making them feel like cattle. From here she was taken to Birkenau where she was assigned to Barrack 12, which was at least similar to her barracks at Westerbork: it contained three levels of bare bunks, flimsy blankets, and freezing cold air. She climbed into the bunk, along with three other women, who were assigned to the same bunk, and instantly collapsed with exhaustion.

When the sirens brutally awoke them the following morning, Caroline felt as though she had only slept for a few minutes. She barely had the strength to get up, but she knew she had to rush outside for roll call. It took more than two hours for the roll to be completed, and most of the women could not wait that long. A number of them fell to their knees or fainted from exhaustion, their lips already a dull blue from the morning's frost. Caroline thought she would be next, but finally, the last name was called and she was directed back to the barracks to eat breakfast. No one dared to approach the prisoners who had been unfortunate enough to fall before the end of the list was reached.

Caroline was ravenously hungry, and ate greedily. Breakfast was meager and stale, but it was the first food she had eaten in days. Again, the siren sounded, followed by yet another roll call. Caroline was assigned to her work group, and armed SS guards with rottweilers escorted them to the site where she would work for the next two months. There, it was her job to ferret out any hidden possessions of value in the prisoners' personal belongings. She was to rip the linings of mountains of old coats in search of money or jewels. She rummaged through packages and suitcases, and any items of value would be gathered in piles, before they were shipped out to Germany. Caroline realized that the owners of these belongings must have been killed. She would come across little reminders of this fact; old photograph fragments in which families smiled happily, dressed in beautiful attire, to celebrate a holiday or family occasion. Wedding photos depressed her most, because naturally, she immediately thought about Soli and her child. Would they ever be lucky enough to pose for a family photograph? Caroline exerted all her effort to fight back the tears that were begging to fall. If she cried, she knew the other women would tell her to stop. They all had to focus on survival, and this work would save their lives, at least for the time being. At least she was sheltered from the cold, and was spared the backbreaking work that other less fortunate women were forced to do, on very little sustenance.

The women were fed watery broth for lunch, then forced to work until dark, when they would be led back to their barracks for yet another roll call. Each roll call was a test of endurance as they lasted for hours. Enduring the roll calls was a torturous process, and many would succumb to their hunger and exhaustion. Those who would try to help their fellow prisoners were severely beaten. Some prisoners opted to end their own pain by running towards the electrified fences that imprisoned them. Suicide was tempting when the alternative was daily torture at the camp.

Caroline quickly learned methods for survival. She became adept at minding her own business, and cultivated silence, so that she wouldn't be tempted to complain. She understood that the camp had only one purpose: to exterminate as many inmates as possible after the last ounce of the prisoners' strength had been expended on forced labor. They were fed three hundred calories of food a day, and the only other option was to eat the vermin that plagued the camp. Caroline knew even the strongest prisoner would succumb. Prisoners would either die from Nazi beatings or malnutrition and infectious diseases. Even though Caroline was painfully aware that her chances of survival were extremely slim, she dared to hope that she would live long enough to see her baby son and husband once the war was over.

A woman named Sara was one of the veterans from Poland. She had been in Auschwitz for over a year, and knew everything there was to know about the camp. One evening a group of women huddled close together as she gave a description of the camp:

"We are located thirty-seven miles west of Cracow, and there is a total camp area of over forty kilometers with a surrounding radius of five kilometers for isolation," she explained. "There are twenty-eight buildings with two stories that make up the camp, which is divided into three sections: Auschwitz One, the base camp and central office, Auschwitz Two, Birkenau, and Auschwitz Three, Monowitz with the subcamp and *buna*. At the entrance to Auschwitz One, there is a sign that reads, '*Arbeit macht frei* [Work makes you free].' These inspiring words are supposed to create the illusion that hard work will result in your liberty. Auschwitz One is the main and smallest part of the camp, consisting of the commandant's office and living quarters, the administration building, the prisoners' kitchen and infirmary, the main guard station, the first crematorium and gas chamber, the Gestapo camp, the group gallows, and the 'death block.' The camp is surrounded by double barbed-wire electric fences and nine watchtowers, so escape is impossible. The 'death block' houses the criminals in the camp. There they have the 'court rooms,' where they torture the prisoners into confession and then 'try' them and sentence them to death. They are then taken outside, where they are lined up against the wall, and are executed. The bodies are dumped in gravel pits around the camp.

"Auschwitz Two, known as Birkenau, was built in March 1942 to accommodate even more prisoners. It is the largest section of Auschwitz. There are 250 barracks, holding up to 1,000 people each, and reaching a peak of 200,000 inmates. There is no running water or sanitary equipment, so disease spreads rapidly. The living quarters and work sites are infested with vermin and insects. This camp consists of the commandant's office, the kitchen barracks, and the terrible 'experimental block,' where medical experiments are conducted on the inmates. There is a storage area which contains the prisoners' personal items. This camp is surrounded by a barbed-wire fence and twenty-eight watchtowers with armed guards.

"Auschwitz Three, known as Monowitz, is a small area that holds the subcamp and the '*buna*.' The main function of this camp is to produce synthetic fuel and rubber. The camp is also used to hold prisoners, due to lack of space in the other sections. Throughout the three camps, there are huge pits that serve as mass graves for thousands of stacked bodies. These graves hold over 100,000 corpses. This way, the executed prisoners cannot be traced or identified. They are lost for eternity."

Caroline and the other new arrivals were grateful to Sara for preparing them mentally. Now they knew exactly what they faced. At the end of

December during a morning roll call, Caroline watched Dr. Mengele appear as the names were called. She watched as he silently indicated with his crop, pointing at the women and making little arcs with the crop in the air, until finally one of the graceful little arcs stopped in front of her.

Chapter 13
Onderduikers

FATHER VERHOEVEN had his hands full trying to locate, and in turn, hide, the growing number of refugees. Each day, the need and danger grew; he had found homes for the starving city children in small country towns where food was still plentiful, and had passed Jews for Protestant refugees. But problems inevitably arose when a refugee accidentally forgot himself, and revealed his Jewish identity; and of course, there was always the risk that someone would trace all these "strays" back to him, and other under-grounders such as Tante Zus. Theo worked hard to disguise his charges, so that they appeared to be exactly who they claimed to be. He became so adept at this kind of work that no one ever felt the need to inform the Nazi authorities when they spotted an unfamiliar child accompanying the nuns or priests into the countryside.

In the openness of their activities, Father Theo knew no one would be able to distinguish the Jewish children from any others. As an added bonus, the communities acknowledged the value and kindness of his work, and many readily volunteered to shelter children to aid him in his efforts.

Providing sustenance for these *onderduikers*, as they were known, was another cause for Theo's concern. At times, Father Theo felt like he was a spy, thief, and smuggler rolled into one. Some of the refugees had no means of self-sufficiency, so they traded their labor for accommodation. Others lived with families who were simply unable to provide this kind of support. For these families, Theo needed to find the necessary funds.

Occasionally, he would also have to help out certain children who seemed ill at ease in their new homes. There was one little Jewish girl, sheltered by the Van Dam family in Eerde, who began to pose a problem when the time came for her to take her First Communion at school. Father Theo quickly found a solution, baptizing the girl in the chapel of the convent of the Sisters of Veghel. Theo ensured that the mother was present at Catholic mass, and provided her with a disguise, so that this was possible. He was reluctant to go ahead with the baptism without the consent of the little girl's mother.

Another embarrassing situation presented itself when a Jewish girl, of about thirteen years of age, attended the high school run by the nuns. One day, the Sister Superior of the school met Theo in the street and said, "Father, we have a city girl who said she is Protestant but she apparently has no knowledge of religious service."

Theo answered, "*Ach*, Sister, in the north there are so many liberal Protestants who don't even baptize their children, denying them any lessons in services or prayer. They figure that when their children reach the age of eighteen, they can make an independent choice whether or not they want to learn Protestantism."

The time came, however, when Theo's works would become too well known for him to feel completely secure. One day, Theo asked an innkeeper near the church if she would rent a spare room out to "a couple from the city," a young couple he wanted to quietly infiltrate into the farming community. She answered him with a stinging reply, saying, "Father, those two are most likely Jews. In my inn, I cannot afford to take such a risk."

Theo protested that his charges were actually a simple Christian couple, Protestants, just like her. All they wanted was a place to live and work in the country, where they would not have to fear persecution from the Nazis because of their opinions.

"You don't fool me, Father," replied the innkeeper. "I know you are hiding Jews. One of my workers, a young girl who comes to sew here, told me so. Around here, everyone knows you have hidden a child with a local family."

Theo pressed her for more information, begging for the name and address of the informer. Theo immediately warned the family who were hiding the child that they were in danger. Within hours, the child was transferred to another home in Schijndel.

Theo came to learn that gossip would make the crucial difference between life and death for so many of the people he was attempting to shelter. He tightened up his communications with his friends in the police force, and tried to stay on top of any similar "stories" circulating inside various communities. One time, a female barber warned him that a couple of farmers waiting to have their hair cut were amiably discussing *onderduikers* in a loud voice. when one said, "*Ja*, we have a great *onderduiker*, he is a great worker." His friend responded, "We could use one like that too, but how do you get one?" "Oh, that's easy," the farmer replied. "Just contact Father Verhoeven, and he will get you one in a jiffy."

In every case, Theo was thankful for the warnings. A good friend, who constantly warned him of pending danger, was Officer Guns of the local police force. As a police officer, he almost always knew in advance about new control systems that the Germans were implementing. An example of his bravery involved an *onderduiker* in Eerde named Janus Verhagen, who fell in love with his neighbor's daughter. The family next door had cooperated with Theo in the past by hosting one of his couriers. Janus had a romance with one of the daughters, and revealed his identity in confidence. Although the family were supportive of Father Theo's efforts, it was crucial that Janus's real identity not be uncovered. Officer Guns quickly warned Theo of the problem. In this case, Arnold and Paula Hoogenhoff resolved the problem. They knew of a place in Horst, in the province of Limburg, where they could find shelter for *onderduikers* at a moment's notice. Paula cycled to Horst, with Janus following behind her at a safe distance. In the event Paula was detained, the *onderduiker* would still have a chance to escape. Only Paula knew the address in Horst by heart, and once the man was safely placed, Paula returned to Veghel by train with the two bicycles.

Most of the *onderduikers* stayed gratis at their addresses, repaying their hosts' kindness by helping with the chores. If money was an issue, the couriers would bring the funds from the city. One problem was the food ration cards, which each *onderduiker* was in need of. In the beginning, these cards were supplied by the Resistance, via Mr. Franssen in Veghel. The Resistance received these cards with the help of courageous officials, however some officials would behave dishonestly, and would ask for more cards than were actually required. As a result, the Resistance decided to control the number of *onderduikers* each official oversaw via the couriers.

For months, Dora Matthijssen had been bringing the ration cards from Amsterdam, but one day, she informed the Resistance that the man who had supplied them with the cards had been caught and shot. She had considered obtaining the ration cards at the legal bureaus, such as the one on St. Oedenrode or on Oss. The numbers of the so-called applications had to be provided every six weeks so that each citizen received their card on time. Dora would have these false application forms printed up in Amsterdam, and Theo would present them at St. Oedenrode or Oss offices, where, because of Theo, there were always several hundred applications too many.

By using a loupe, Theo was able to detect that the first batch that Dora had brought was false, but the second time, it was perfect. He could not personally go each month to collect these three hundred cards, sixty for his organization and two hundred and forty for the Amsterdam area. Luckily, two sisters from Veghel worked at the distribution offices in St. Oedenrode. They were prepared to bring the cards to Veghel, with the understanding that these cards were designated for *onderduikers*, and were to be picked up at their Veghel home by Theo. Apparently the sisters never knew that these cards were false, although they probably suspected that they were stolen.

It once happened that the sisters did not have enough cards, so they returned a hundred application forms to Theo, that did not have the same numbers that he had given. His colleague Father Willibrord went to Oss to exchange them there in the names of the hundred students interned with the Fathers in Veghel. Dora, on the other hand, would return each time to Amsterdam and would put her ration cards in a separate attaché case, while carrying her personal belongings in another small case. The secret case would be loaded onto the train, directly on to the baggage net above the passengers. Should there be a control in the train, no one in the cabin knew who the case belonged to, and no one would have suspected Dora, since she was already carrying a case with her personal belongings.

It happened on one occasion, while changing trains in Boxtel for Amsterdam, that the entire station was encircled for a "control" action. Everyone was holding their baggage in their hands, including Dora. She spotted a young German officer, also waiting for the train, and managed to prevent the inspection, by flirting with the man. Dora placed the suitcase on the ground next to him, and started talking to him. When she saw the inspectors approaching, she told the officer that she had to go to the toilet for a moment. The suitcase stood near the unsuspecting officer. When the danger had passed, Dora reemerged, thanked the officer warmly, and boarded the train.

Things seemed to be going fairly well for Theo, until one day, the head of the distribution office, Mr. Helmonds, came to Father Verhoeven's monastery, and asked to see the rector. Luckily, he was unavailable, so Brother Willibrord, a friend of Father Verhoeven, took his place. Mr. Helmonds had come to warn them that there were false cards constantly being issued, and the person responsible apparently belonged to this monastery. Upon the rector's return to the monastery, he was informed about Mr. Helmond's visit. In the meantime, Brother Willibrord informed Theo of this latest development. At lunchtime, the rector asked for silence to discuss a very serious complaint. One of the brothers was apparently taking hundreds of ration cards illegally, and due to the seriousness of the matter, he would now openly ask each and every person present to give account.

"Father De Lange, do you know anything about this matter?"

The brother responded, "No, rector."

"Father Verhoeven, do you know anything about this matter?"

Theo answered, "No, rector."

No one admitted knowledge of the illegal ration cards, but it had become clear that the risk was becoming increasingly great. In Amsterdam there was a Jewish pregnant woman, an *ondergedooken*, whose husband had been deported and never returned. Since the neighbors were suspicious, there could be no sounds of crying babies. As soon as she gave birth, the baby would have to be moved, or mother and child would need to be relocated together. Theo's group was approached to see if they could place a newborn baby. At night in bed, Theo was inspired with a wonderful idea. He instantly thought of the Braat family. He had never been to their home, but he knew that they had been married a long time and did not have any children. The next morning, before he was due to give his lecture, he tried to convince the Braats to shelter the baby. The Braats did, in fact, want a child, but one of their own, however they agreed to adopt a four-day-old baby. When they heard that it was a Jewish baby, they were momentarily frightened. But Theo, with his charm, managed to convince them of the great deed they were performing, and ended his visit by telling them, "Now all your efforts should result in the acceptance of your prayers."

Ten months later, Mrs. Braat had two children in her arms, a Jewish child, who they had named Leontiene, and her own child, though neither of the two could walk just yet. (Miraculously, Leontiene was reunited with her biological mother in 1946.)

Theo Verhoeven summarized the wartime years in the following way:

"It was a nerve-wracking experience: first, I would lecture, then in the evening, I would cycle around the area, visiting the *onderduikers*, solving the problems that constantly arose, searching for new addresses, with all the risks involved, which made you that much more nervous. Sometimes you couldn't sleep from fear, and would end up sleeping over at friends' house, for comfort. Colleagues considered you to be a difficult, prickly man. Was it any wonder? You had to keep everything secret for the sake of your superiors, who would be arrested if there were any slip-ups. The rector caught me off guard, because somehow he had found out the truth. I told him that I had to live with my conscience, and therefore did what I did.

"Later Father Boumans was picked up by the Germans, because he had violated the German's strict prohibition against owning a radio. A German police officer appeared at the door of the Blue Kei, and warned the rector that if anyone else was caught violating the rules, the whole mission would be closed down. That is all we needed!"

Risks constantly presented themselves, and Theo was never free from danger. He and his colleagues never wrote anything down, and committed hundreds of names and addresses to memory rather than risk the whole operation to the sudden discovery of lists of names and addresses or any other evidence. Theo's life had become a terrifying and demanding juggling act, one that could end catastrophically if the wrong information was mentioned to the wrong person. Theo could never breathe easy, but he had no choice. He would not have been able to live with himself had he acted apathetically.

Chapter 14
Experiments in Block 10

Winter, 1943–1945

THE FIRST TIME Caroline laid eyes on one of the women emerging from Experiment Block 10, she felt like she was about to vomit. The women were scarred and burned; they had been tortured slowly, yet they somehow continued to live, in spite of their agony. Their eyes were encircled by bloody, bruised marks, and their expressions were vacant. Some of the women had been beaten so many times that they could barely stand, and Caroline wondered how human beings could physically endure such beatings. Some had fresh amputation wounds where they'd once had limbs. After being selected by Dr. Mengele, Caroline could only assume that she would suffer the same torturous experiences as the others. For the next couple of days, she was well fed, housed in slightly better living quarters, but inside, was numb with denial.

On her third day in the block, she was led to a brightly lit room in the basement of one of the camp's larger buildings. There, the unthinkable, yet undeniable, experiments began. Nothing could have prepared her for what she was about to endure. Strapped onto the gurney, and injected with unknown solutions, she screamed until she became unconscious. After the convulsions were induced, the length of her consciousness was recorded: this was the goal of the experiment. When all the data was recorded, her tormentors led her out to her quarters. Dr. Slavka, a Russian prisoner recruited by the Nazis to help with the experiments, looked into Caroline's eyes when she awoke.

When the Russian doctor spoke, she calmed Caroline with her soft and soothing voice. She spoke sweetly to Caroline while carefully changing the dressings on her wounds. "*Du must mut haben,*" she repeated to her in German, "you must have faith."

Caroline smelled a faint antiseptic odor in the cream Dr. Slavka applied to her wounds, a familiar scent that reminded her of hospitals. The soft, sweet murmurs and the warmth of the recovery room finally lulled Caroline into an exhausted sleep. This was the first time since she had arrived in Auschwitz that anyone had shown her any compassion or concern. As she became stronger, her morale was raised each time the doctor stopped by to pay her a visit. The strange Dr. Slavka was the only person to treat Caroline with tenderness, yet she was aware on another level of the reality of the doctor's work. She could not reconcile in her mind how the doctor could be so kind and caring, on the one hand, yet inflict such torture, on the other. Dr. Slavka's bedside manner was enticing, especially after months of deprivation, but she was sickened by the thought that she was relying on her tormentor for care.

When Mengele wanted to see Caroline himself, she imagined every conceivable horror as she was escorted by the guard to his office. Mengele disarmed her fear: he motioned her to sit down in the soft, cushioned office chair, and smiled sweetly at her while she spoke. She watched him closely for any quick movements, any break in the facade of a gentlemanly demeanor.

He sat at his desk in a perfectly pressed uniform, smelling sweetly of a mixture of sandalwood and tobacco, coffee and leather. Not once did he display the ferocious cruelty that made him infamous. Mengele was a good-looking man with a gentle voice, full of compliments and wit. He gazed at Caroline intently as she spoke, impressed by her composure and command of the German language. He asked her how she had found the experiments and asked many questions concerning her family's health, as well as her reactions to the injections she had received. Then he asked her about her sexual experiences: what had she done, with whom, and what were her sexual preferences. Caroline wanted to vomit with rage at his intrusion, knowing that his perverted mind was reenacting all the sexual scenarios that she was forced to describe, but she realized that if she wanted to stay alive, she had to give him some answers.

Finally, the interrogation stopped, and Mengele served Caroline coffee from a gleaming silver tray, along with crème-filled wafer biscuits in a small porcelain dish. Again, he had hidden his wolf-like interior behind the genteel facade of the gracious host. She could see from his manner that when he was with her, he played the gallant gentleman, and acknowledged that Mengele's attraction to her could bring her some reprieve. Caroline suddenly felt dizzy from the scent of the drink.

He encouraged her, saying, "Drink, please. Enjoy." She finally lifted the cup to her lips and savored the hot liquid.

"I am sorry to hear about the loss of your child," he said, and then added, "that will be all for today. You are dismissed."

Caroline finished her coffee and gently placed it back on the saucer. She resolved not to tell anyone about her meeting with Mengele, as she wanted to wait and see what would happen next. The next day, Caroline and the other inmates were standing outside in the cold briskness of the morning air, surrounding a huge bonfire of burning wood that provided the shivering women with delicious warmth. No one had prevented them from standing near it, so the women took advantage of the opportunity to bask in the glowing comfort of the fire. Suddenly Mengele arrived on the scene. Everyone immediately backed away from the fire, and retreated from the approaching SS officers, who were accompanying Mengele. After several minutes, eleven dump trucks, filled with children, arrived. The trucks drew closer to the fire while SS officers circled around the flames. Mengele stood back to issue commands to his officers, and watched silently as children were thrown by the officers into the flames. The screams were deafening; several children tried to crawl away from the flames and run to safety. A group of officers, armed with sticks, moved towards the fire, and mercilessly pushed the children back into the flames. Hours passed as more and more children were flung onto the pyre. More officers were dispatched to watch over the women, who were forced to watch the burning of live children. Deafening screams echoed throughout the camp, until the last of the doomed children perished. Caroline knew that their screams would haunt her for as long as she lived.

Mengele beamed with pleasure at the response of the imprisoned women. He performed his work with relish, evidently, and enjoyed both the execution and the expression of horror on the faces of the onlookers. Caroline no longer fooled herself about Mengele's supposed charm – he was a ruthless and cold-blooded murderer, who did not possess an ounce of human compassion. He was power-hungry, and thrived on the knowledge that he could cause destruction and havoc amongst innocent victims. As long as he had his troop of armed SS militia behind him, he could indulge any sadistic whim in the camp. It was hard to tell whether the war had created a person like Mengele or whether Mengele had created the war with his own warped psyche. It didn't matter to Caroline. All she knew was that the torture was not about to stop.

Caroline was correct in her assessment: the experiments and torture continued. With each round, she underwent the now familiar routine of cruelty laced with kindness. Each time she endured a new round of torture, she was fed with better food – cuts of meat, for example, and vegetables served with butter; just enough to restore her strength and allow her to survive the next battery of viral injections or induced convulsions. Weeks passed in this way, with no change in the routine.

She had learned from the kapos that Soli was still alive and had been put to work in a fuel and rubber plant. The news about Soli was the only ray of sunshine in Caroline's dark, blighted existence. Mengele checked in on Caroline from time to time, and brought her gifts of sweets. His compassion was so convincing, that she almost always was taken in by his charm, but was cruelly jolted back to reality when she witnessed his inhuman viciousness. She had to remind herself over and over again of his split personality; he had a Jekyll and Hyde character type, going from one radical extreme to another. Only days earlier, she was privy to Mengele's violent mood swings. Some women in the yard were loaded on to the truck, to be taken to the gas chambers. Mengele stood watching, happily whistling a tune by Wagner, when he saw one of the women trying to escape from the truck. This act of defiance provoked instant rage in Mengele, and he turned into a wild beast. He grabbed the woman by the neck, and began to beat her head to a bloody pulp, all the while shouting at the top of his voice, "You want to escape, you dirty, filthy Jew, you are going to burn and fry like the others."

Horrified, Caroline watched the woman's beautiful eyes turn into an ugly mass of blood, her nose was broken, and she was tossed back onto the truck half-dead. Mengele then proceeded to the corner where there was a sink, and with a smile of satisfaction, he washed his hands. This person, who resembled a handsome movie star, and had a disarming smile, suddenly transformed into a murderous barbarian, who was only satisfied once he had indulged his sadistic urges.

The camp was supervised by the six thousand SS members and selected prisoners called kapos, and by sonderkommandos, who operated in the camp's crematoria. Most of the sonderkommandos were ultimately killed, to ensure that no one outside of the camp ever discovered what really went on. The murdered sonderkommandos were quickly replaced by newly selected prisoners. As hard as the Nazis tried to keep the gas chambers a secret, there was not one person in the camp who did not know what caused the terrible smell emitted by the chimneys. The kapos were the ones most feared by the prisoners, as a few of these were Jews, while most were Germans. The kapos comprised of conmen, convicted murderers, petty criminals, and former soldiers, and they were contemptuous of the Jews even though they were also victims of Nazi cruelty. Many felt superiority over the Jews, as they were spared the gas chambers, which were reserved for gypsies and Jews alone.

Caroline had encountered two decent kapos, one by the name of Samuel, and a Czech called Jan. Jan wore a red triangle with a capital P, the mark of a political prisoner. Both were kind to her, occasionally smuggling some extra food and, once, a cigarette. Jan and Samuel often told her about what they had seen while they worked. All of them were fascinated with Mengele's dual nature, and they often related stories of his vicious, volatile temper getting the better of him. During one such meeting with these two kapos, on January 17, 1944, Caroline learned that Soli, her husband, her true love, had died. Jan had motioned to her that he wanted to speak to her privately, and informed her that he had been gassed in Monowitz the day before.

For the first time, Caroline lost all hope for her own survival. She sobbed and sobbed until there were no tears left. She could not envisage life without Soli, he was her rock, the one who made everything look so much brighter, and without him, she did not want to continue living. She became one of the "undead" among the prisoners. She lived as if in a trance. In her mind, she was warm and protected, surrounded by her brothers and sisters and her lovely, healthy baby. Reality, the cruel and painful place filled with daily tortures and experiments, no longer existed for her. She was so numb inside that she did not even feel the pain of the countless experiments she was forced to endure. She stopped reacting to the world around her, which piqued the curiosity of the doctors even more. Perhaps it is fair to say that it was their curiosity that kept her alive. Physically, she was kept alive because she did not react to the experiments; emotionally, she was as dead as if she had succumbed to one of them. She no longer had an identity.

Eva Kraus, a twenty-eight-year-old Polish woman, who shared her bunk with Caroline, saved her. Eva was persistent in her efforts to revive Caroline, taking care of her after she was brought back to the bunk after each round of experiments, and massaging her back to a kind of renewed strength. They quickly became "camp sisters," who looked after each other, no matter what. Once again, Caroline slowly began to harbor new hopes for her survival, and clung to the image of her son as a reason to stay alive. Eva herself endured her share of torture and Caroline worked to restore her spirits. On one occasion, Caroline comforted Eva when she was in excruciating pain from injections to her ovaries. Eva suffered severe burning sensations all over her body and Caroline held her and tried to soothe her pain with calming words. For the first time, Caroline felt as though she was really needed. It was this mutual support that revived Caroline from the "undead," and gave her a purpose to live.

When Eva recuperated, she would tell Caroline about her village, and her father, the ritual slaughterer, a very learned and pious Jew. Eva came from an Orthodox Jewish home and her powerful faith in God amazed Caroline. Eva prayed several times a day and tried to convince Caroline that God would save them from their humiliation and degradation. Caroline had long ago forgotten God, in her attempt, for so many months, to survive by instinct. Eva awakened Caroline to her spiritual needs, and inspired her to believe in God again. She focused her thoughts again on her baby, and kept up her struggle for his sake, with God's help. Caroline told Eva how beautiful the last Passover Seder had been at her in-laws' home, before all this pain and suffering began. That night she dreamed of the family gathering at the Seder table, and imagined Soli in her arms again. There is no doubt that each one helped the other to survive these horrifying months.

In October of 1944, Caroline was forced to stand in a vat of ice water for a number of hours so that the doctors could study how the human body can survive freezing temperatures in water. The Nazis conducted this research so that they could calculate the survival time of navy crews or pilots left to float in a frozen sea after a plane wreck.

Mengele served Caroline some hot chicken soup after the experiment, and conducted himself in his usual manner. He was impressed with her endurance, and admired her strength. She ate the steaming broth quickly, then waited for him to dismiss her so she could return to her bunk as usual.

That night, as Caroline shivered in Eva's arms, Eva told her about the revolt in the crematorium that had taken place several days earlier. Eva talked about Rosa Robota, a Polish Jew who worked in the clothing supply section of the camp. Rosa and another prisoner, Noah Zabladowicz, had plotted the revolt together. Rosa had obtained explosives from friends in the Union Munitions plant in Auschwitz, and worked with some other partisans to make bombs from tin cans and gunpowder. The bombs would be used to blow up the crematoria and the gas chambers; this was the Jews' only hope for survival. Noah and Rosa both knew the war would end soon, and the Nazis realized they were fighting a losing battle, but they were determined to eliminate as much of European Jewry as possible. To this end, they had increased their gassings so that the chambers were active day and night, murdering thousands upon thousands. The bombing of the crematoria was their only chance for survival.

Rosa and several dozen women smuggled in the explosive powder, and helped Timofei Borodin, a Russion POW munitions expert, make the bombs out of sardine cans. The sonderkommandos then hid the explosives in the carts used to haul the corpses out of the chambers. On October 4, 1944, as planned, Crematorium IV was bombed with the homemade explosives, and so began the revolt. Five SS men were killed, and several were injured in the pandemonium, while six hundred sonderkommandos escaped through the wires. Many were caught and killed, unable to escape the well-armed Nazi presence. A special team from the Gestapo was brought in to investigate the revolt. The explosives were traced back to the Union plant and several suspects were rounded up; they were tortured until they confessed. They named Rosa Robota as the organizer, and identified her accomplices as Regina Safirsztain, Ella Gartner, and Estucia Wajcblum, who had all helped smuggle the explosives to the crematorium. Rosa was instantly arrested.

Because of his connections, Noah Zabladowicz was able to visit Rosa in her prison cell. Noah was worried that Rosa would disclose information under torture, but was relieved to hear that Rosa had not said a word.

He found her writhing on the filthy floor, half-dead, moaning softly. She gathered her strength to tell Noah what her torturers had done to her. He could not conceive how she had endured such torture without betraying her comrades. She begged Noah to continue resisting the Nazis, despite such terrible consequences. Rosa was twenty-three years old when she and her three comrades were hanged before the camp population. Her last words were "*hazak v'amatz,* Be strong and brave." Thanks to Rosa and her companions, the Crematoria had been so badly damaged by the bombing that the gassing stopped, and as a result, groups were sent by train to Bergen Belsen, where some of these prisoners survived, due to the liberation of the camp, several weeks later.

In late December 1944, Caroline contracted typhus. She was not even aware that the new year had come in, and she entered 1945 in a state of feverish delirium. Eva ran off to find one of the prisoner doctors to help her. Fortunately for her, the Allied Forces were closing in on the camp. Mengele and his cohorts were now occupied with working out an evacuation plan. As the Soviets approached, the Nazis organized their own escape from Auschwitz. They tried to burn down Block 10 before the Soviets arrived.

THE FINAL RESISTANCE

Chapter 15
Resistance in Veghel, 1944

THE GOLDEN LION HOTEL in Veghel had become a busy place lately. By day, it was a bustling restaurant and bar; by night, the cellar was filled with *onderduikers* and Allied air-crew members, eating and drinking under the noses of the Nazis. Bertie Fox certainly had courage. He was a professional hotelier who offered a first-class service, and was admired by Dutch and German clients.

Aside from the huge risk he was taking fostering a Jewish child, Bertie also supported his wife's cousin, Tilly Sevriens, in all her resistance work. Tilly had started out in early 1943 with the "LO," the Land Organization for Dutch *onderduikers*, an official resistance group. The primary goal of the LO was the protection and distribution of *onderduikers*. They also produced counterfeit coupons, and obtained authentic coupons from loyal Dutch citizens employed by the Nazis. They kept an eye on Dutch collaborators and maintained good relations with members of the police force, who would tip them off before an arrest of an *onderduiker* was about to occur.

Tilly had been very busy arranging addresses for *onderduikers*, and was also responsible for looking after the escapees in transit, who sought overnight refuge in the hotel's cellar. In January 1944, Sjeff de Groot, an old acquaintance who had previously run an excellent falsification service in The Hague, visited Tilly. Sjeff had recently been appointed leader of KP

Noord Brabant Oost, a coordinated armed resistance in the area, and had succeeded in uniting all renegade groups under one umbrella.

One of these groups in the Veghel area operated under Theo van Schijndel, whose *nom de guerre* was "Sjors." Sjeff asked Tilly directly if she was willing to help Sjors in the field, as they were short of female operatives who moved freely and less conspicuously among the Nazi troops. He made it clear to her that while the LO maintained a low profile, the Central Government Fighting Group "KP" carried out sabotage operations at the local level. The KP attacked targets in and around Veghel, such as railroad tracks, telegraph and telephone lines, German supply points, and motor pools. He continued, telling her that they were cooperating closely with MI9, the British Military Intelligence Section, which had been set up to coordinate with Dutch resistance networks to assist Allied airmen shot down over Holland to return to Britain. They had parachuted some agents into Holland who had linked up with their organization, and had brought them money, maps, and false papers to assist the airmen. Sjeff concluded his explanation by telling her, "So as you can see, this is no picnic. You might want to think about the danger you would be exposed to."

Tilly did not have to think, her adrenaline was pumping and she could feel her heart pounding away with excitement. "Count me in," she said. "What's the next move?"

"You will meet with Sjors at his headquarters at Johan van Genugten on the Koeverine near St. Oedenrode," Sjeff answered. "There you will join with your local friends Ad and Ton Kuyper to make further arrangements."

With a kiss and hug they parted, and so began a new chapter in Tilly's life.

In the early morning of February 12, 1944, Tilly was feeding Jantje a soft-boiled egg when Bertie burst into the kitchen. "Did you hear the latest news?" he asked.

"No," answered Tilly. "What's happened?"

"There is a tremendous fire raging at the distribution center right here in Veghel, the firemen have been working for over an hour, and the word is that it might be sabotage!"

Tilly wiped Jantje's chin, which was now bright yellow from the yolk of the egg, and smiled at the baby. She thought how glad she was that her efforts with the KP had paid off, as now they had in their possession all the distribution cards they had stolen before setting the building ablaze. She lovingly played with Jantje, who smiled and ate his breakfast, basking in her attention. During the next few days, a group of Germans from the *Sicherheitsdienst*, the security police, in Eindhoven came to investigate the incidents leading up to the fire, but finding no cause, they attributed it to careless smoking. On Tuesday afternoon, another fire raged in Veghel at the Van Coenen-Schoenmakers factory. The Wehrmacht's entire stock of one thousand tons of hay and seventy tons of oats were destroyed in the blaze. This time the investigation continued for weeks, as the Nazis suspected sabotage. Of course, with all their suspicions, they would never have suspected that the grains had, in fact, been distributed among the farmers who worked with the resistance.

Tilly carefully listened in on the conversations she overheard between the Nazi customers in the café, and then reported back to Sjors. She also informed him about the NSB officer who helped the Nazis with their investigations. The group had a serious setback on the night of May 13, when Sjors was arrested along with his chauffeur. They had been preparing to target a Wehrmacht warehouse, and while doing so, fell into a cunning trap set by the Nazis. Unfortunately, Tilly did not overhear such conversations in her restaurant, so Sjors had no way of knowing what lay ahead. That night, Sjors and his chauffeur were taken to the German security offices in Hertogenbosch. They were in deep trouble, as both of them were armed and Sjors had in his possession some important documents.

Strangely enough, when they arrived, Sjors managed to rid himself of the documents and the Germans never found any trace of them. Tilly found out that the local policeman, Officer Guns (a pseudonym), played an important role in the disappearance of these documents. After several days, Sjors was transferred to the notorious prison at Vught. Sjeff de Groot appointed in Sjor's place Gijs Bossert as leader of the Veghel-Eerde KP group. Gijs had been hiding in Veghel for several months with false papers. His brother Ko also lived in Veghel. Gijs who had been detained, and was on his way to being interrogated, narrowly escaped from a train and landed in Eerde to hide in Harry Ruys's farm. Harry was well known in the area, both for his farming and his cooperation with the Resistance.

Through Father Willenborg, Gijs became actively involved in several sabotage attacks against Nazi installations. He frequented the Golden Lion, where he would secretly pass instructions to Tilly. Tilly had befriended

Ann Peters and Wim Korsten, who were in the position, as local telephone operators, to overhear all conversations; as a result, anything of importance was related to Tilly, who in turn informed the group. Ann and Wim made sure that the group had telephone contact even during the most difficult times. In the first days of September, Sjeff de Groot told Tilly that Sjors had been executed at the Vught camp in August.

"More reason to continue our struggle against these bastards," Tilly responded. He then informed her that there would be a massive invasion very soon by allied forces and that he had received the green light from the British government to sabotage the railway and telephone lines between Eerde and Boxtels. They were to damage any German vehicle in the vicinity by pouring sugar or salt in the gas and oil tanks. The men would take care of the railway lines, while Tilly and another female courier called Greetje Van As, would go out on their bikes at night, and wreak as much havoc as possible.

Over the next few days, the men axed telephone poles and scattered toothed steel bars on the roads to rupture the tires of German cars, as they travelled along the popular highway. Tilly and Greetje tallied up the sixty-two vehicles they had treated to salt and sugar, and rode home whistling happily. The next assignment order by Sjeff was more of a challenge: to derail the trains while stealing the weapons and ammunition that were being stored inside.

On the night of September 4, Tilly accompanied the group so that she could watch out for anyone coming, and sound the alarm in case of danger. While she stayed in the car near the railtrack, Gijs and Gerrit Mobers, Janus van de Meerakker, and Bart van Roosmalen, well-known members of the Resistance in Veghel, got to work on the tracks. Tilly had a perfect view of everything around her as it was a clear night. She could see the men struggling with the heavy bolts and screws that held the rails in place, and could even hear their grunts and their expressions of relief when they finally succeeded. They heard a train approaching from Boxtel, and they all quickly dove into the dunes behind a beet patch. Slowly the train approached; they could see that it was transporting wounded German soldiers. The men lay still. Under the dyke, the connecting rail still held, and the train continued on its way toward Heimat, uninterrupted. After renewing their efforts zealously, they managed to bend the rails aside, and insert a steel pipe between the bent rails. It was already past 4:00 A.M., and

Tilly was becoming restless and tired. She heard another train approaching from Veghel. As the train reached the spot that the men had just left, it derailed with an enormous noise. Sparks from the screeching rails flew in all directions. This train, it turned out, had been loaded with all sorts of military equipment.

Later that morning, Gijs Bossert went to assess the damage. Railroad employees were busy repairing the damage, and several German soldiers, with rifles slung over their shoulders, were patrolling the area around the train. At one point, all the guards gathered around the locomotive to talk. Gijs wasted no time – he jumped on one of the cars, and swiftly cut through the iron cable with his pliers, releasing the door. He stole an iron chest that looked like a valise and made his escape silently, running with the chest through the fields to Harry Ruys's farm. There he hid the chest in the pile of manure, making a mental note of its label. It read, "Twenty-four spring hand grenades."

Tilly's neighbor a few doors down from the hotel was Ton Kuyper. Ton's home was the central point of the Veghel group. Behind their bicycle store was a huge yard, which they used to conceal weapons, gasoline, and all kinds of metals that might be needed at any given moment. Like Tilly, Ton was involved with all the organizations in the area. He would pedal to Den Bosch, Eindhoven, and the entire region, to conduct his work in complete secrecy. Ton helped Father Verhoeven deliver bicycles to his *onderduikers* at the required meeting place. He was in contact with the LO branch in Veghel through Frans Nuchelmans, another well-known local figure, and cooperated with Tilly at all times.

Pa Kuyper, the head of the Kuyper clan, was the postmaster in Veghel. All the mail passed through his hands and was screened, including the mail that was directed to the German authorities or NSB members. In screening the mail, Kuyper's group came across a letter written by an NSB member to Sicherheitsdienst security service in Hertogenbosch, denouncing the activities of the Kuyper family. This letter was full of detailed information about the arms cache kept by Ton's family, as well as a list of all Tilly Sevriens' activities within the LO at the Golden Lion in Veghel. The letter even went so far as to reveal that the Golden Lion was a cover for Underground activity, as well as being a shelter for many refugees hiding from the Nazis. Everyone in the group understood that in a small community such as Veghel, there was little privacy. No matter how discreet or silent an operation was, the risk of being found out was great. Living with this situation, day in day out, caused great strain and stress to all members of the Resistance. It was a fact of life one had to contend with, but nevertheless, each time the group encountered hitches such as these, it still came as a great shock. The letter was promptly destroyed, and the writer mysteriously disappeared the following day.

On the night of September 8, Gijs once again led the group on an action, with Tilly as the lookout. With the stolen hand grenades, Gijs managed to construct a bomb, which was placed underneath the rails, halfway from the Eerde station to Schijndel. Gijs ordered everyone to take cover as he pulled the string, setting off the explosion. A rain of stones and sand poured over them all; a huge hole in the rails was visible. Quickly, they dispersed. The next day, the following notice was posted everywhere:

PUBLIC NOTICE: *Last night, from the 8th to the 9th of September 1944, in the trackway of Schijndel-Veghel, a railway track was blown up. The German station chief in Boxtel, in presence of a Hauptman deer Wehrmacht, orders the mayors of Veghel and Schijndel as follows: As of today, 9 September, twenty citizens must present themselves every evening at 9 o'clock (21:00 hours) from each municipality of Schijndel and Veghel, and under police escort, enter the police stations of Schijndel and Veghel. The police will accompany the twenty citizens to the rail line Schijndel-Veghel to guard from 22:00 until five o'clock the next morning.*

The foreseen declared punishment: One man out of ten, one woman out of fifty, and one child out of a hundred – one hundred of them will be shot and then hung in the marketplace. After eight o'clock, no one is allowed on the street, otherwise five houses will be set on fire. The citizen guards must be of the ages between 25 and 35 years, and must be known as the richest and most respected citizens. In relation to the seriousness of the circumstances, and in the interest of the whole population, I am relying on the fact that everyone will abide by these valid rules and will be adhered to the letter by each individual.

Veghel, 9 September 1944, the Mayor of Veghel

The following day another notice circulated:

PUBLIC NOTICE: *By order of the local commandant of the Duitsche Wehrmacht, I make the following known: in the event of damage to, destruction and disappearance of, any traffic signs, road indicators, or direction indicators, five of the best-known citizens will be hanged at the market, as punishment. Furthermore, all other actions, conducted against the interests of the Duitsche Wehrmacht, or against the German Republic, such as disappearance or destruction of German military or other goods, will be punished very severely. I trust, in view of the serious situation, that everyone, young or old, will abstain from EACH sabotage effort.*

Veghel, 10 September 1944, the Mayor of Veghel

Needless to say, these placards caused great unrest among the population. Tilly and her companions held an emergency meeting, in which they were ordered by the leader of the Brabant resistance to cease all sabotage activities immediately. The plans to blow up a railway bridge near Veghel were scrapped. Sjeff and his group refrained from involvement in any activity that could provoke the Nazis to carry out their reprisals against the civilian population. All agreed it would be irresponsible to risk the lives of innocent citizens with liberation so close. Instead, everyone prepared for the moment the Nazis would be removed from power, as that day appeared to be coming soon. But suddenly, someone threatened to put a spoke in the wheel: an *onderduiker* in Eerde went to Marinus the silversmith, to borrow tools, which apparently were materials for destroying railway equipment. Sjeff was immediately informed, and he received orders that this man should be stopped from carrying out his plan at all costs, even if it required using force. Albert, one of the group's participants later told the group how it ended.

"As instructed by Sjeff, I went to the address of the *onderduiker*. He was not home, and after inquiring as to his whereabouts, I was told that he was at his next-door neighbors' house. I found him there and asked him what he intended to do with the tools he had borrowed from Marinus. He replied that it was none of my business. I then confronted him with my suspicions that he was about to commit an act of sabotage on the railway lines, and that I could not permit this to take place, not under any circumstances. When I asked him to return the tools to Marinus, and leave the railway lines alone, he reacted very angrily. He felt excluded, as he was never asked to join the resistance to help in earlier sabotages. I then threatened him with force if he would not comply with my demands. He then said that we should go and discuss this with the local priest, Father Jos Willenborg.

"I went by bike, while he was on foot, which gave me the chance to inform the priest of the situation before he arrived. The priest asked me to remain for the discussion. Together we put pressure on him until he agreed to return the tools to Marinus."

Luckily, liberation was soon to come, just a few days later.

Chapter 16
Death March

FOR THE FIRST TIME, Caroline could see the Germans losing their grip on Europe. News of the imminent end of the war was spreading rapidly, and it was evident that the Germans' military force was steadily deteriorating. The prisoners at the camp knew that the Allied armies were approaching, and could smell liberation in the air. Caroline allowed herself to entertain dreams of reuniting with her baby. It was a small luxury, but it sustained her more than anything else. It was common knowledge that the Soviets were expected to arrive at Auschwitz any day now, so the SS and camp personnel were anxious to transfer as soon as possible the prisoners out of Auschwitz to the forced labor camps in Germany proper. Without any prior notice, sixty thousand prisoners were rounded up, and marched into Wodzislaw in the western part of upper Silesia. Once again, they were loaded into ramshackle train cars, and transported to yet another camp.

Caroline and Eva were part of the transfer, and embarked on their journey with almost no clothing, and no flesh on their bones to provide them with insulation against the cold. The snow on the ground was still fresh, and the wind was bitter. Caroline became so sick and incoherent that she stopped wondering when she would next eat; however, despite her growing weakness, she made every effort to keep up with Eva. This was just as well, as those who could not keep up with the rest of the group were unceremoniously shot. Eva understood how determined the Nazis were to prevent liberation of the prisoners by the Allied troops. Although she was weak herself, she supported Caroline in her sickness, and made sure that she kept up with the others.

By the second day, they were placed on a transport. Eva was grateful, even if it was in a cattle car on the train. As soon as they reached the German lines, though, they were all expected to get out and march again. Caroline could not bring herself to continue, and Eva was beginning to flail from exhaustion herself.

"What's the point of this?" asked Caroline. "I'll only get us both killed if you keep pulling me along. I have to stay here."

She knew that she was suffering from the camp's own epidemic of typhus, and though she wanted to believe she could struggle and survive, Caroline knew her chances were poor.

"Save yourself, Eva," she said, in the hope that her friend would find some strength to continue on their journey.

Eva gently led her to a piece of snow-covered ground, away from the group of marching prisoners; she hoped that the guard would not notice them. Caroline could just see the ice-covered boots of the guard march towards her as she let herself lose consciousness. The guard held his gun down toward her body, and poked at her stomach. Caroline was already unable to feel anything. When she did not react, he tried again. Another two SS guards approached. One cocked his rifle at her as she lay in the snow, smiling at the thought of pulling the trigger.

"Wait," said one of the other guards, "It would be a pity to waste a bullet on a Jewish bitch. She's dead anyway."

Eva watched the spectacle, and uttered a silent, thankful prayer as the guards walked away from Caroline's body. All around her, the German countryside lay still under the soft white blanket of the newly fallen snow. The quiet fields lay empty as the winter darkness began to descend. In this stillness, Fritz, an Austrian farmer, was making his way home on his horse and wagon. Before him, all was white with the new snow, showing no trace of the hundreds of pairs of feet that were forced to trudge through the area earlier in the day.

He did notice, however, a dark spot in the whiteness, and as he drew close, he discerned the form of a human being. He climbed down from his cart and attempted to find a pulse in the woman's wrist. Quickly, he lifted her onto the straw cart, and tried to warm her. Her body was as light as a feather. He urged his horse to go on, as he still was a long way from home.

When Caroline opened her eyes again, she was lying in a warm room with a crucifix on the wall. The sheets on her bed were crisp and white, and she was wearing a new nightgown that smelled of laundry detergent. She had been scrubbed and was finally free of the lice that had plagued her, ever since the beginning of her incarceration. Someone had apparently washed and disinfected her. Her throat ached, and she was feverish and weak, but she was alive. On the nightstand beside her stood a pitcher of water and a glass. She tried to get up, but could not find the strength. She collapsed into the soft bed, and wondered about the train of events that had led her to this haven. When she tried to speak, she was disappointed to find that even that was too much for her. All she could do was sink back, ponder, and wait. The house she was in had to belong to someone, she reasoned, so it would only be a matter of time before she would find out what had happened to her. Finally, after what felt like hours, she heard the door creak open and watched as a woman pushed it open a few inches to peek inside. The woman smiled when Caroline met her eyes and ventured into the room.

"Don't be scared," she murmured in German. "You are safe here."

Caroline managed to whisper, "Water, please," and was grateful as the lady poured the drink into a glass, and held it while she took small sips.

"My name is Mitzi," she said, preempting Caroline's question. "My husband Fritz found you dying in the snow. You have been here for ten days, and have been treated by our doctor. You were very ill."

Caroline was too weak to ask any questions, and continued to drink, while Mitzi explained the situation.

"Just rest, now, and don't worry," she repeated. "I'm sure you could use a little bit of soup."

Caroline watched as Mitzi left the room, then eagerly returned with a tray, and placed it on Caroline's lap. She dipped the spoon into the hot liquid and held it up to Caroline's mouth.

"Eat, please," she said, while Caroline tried to cooperate.

Mitzi had a soothing voice, and chatted quietly while Caroline ate, knowing that this poor woman must have so many questions that needed answering. She told Caroline about herself and Fritz, her husband, and their small farm, where they raised cows and chickens. Their son was missing in action somewhere in Russia. Mitzi was quick to reassure Caroline that they were not Nazis. Their son had gone off to fight for the Germans in the war, affording them a great deal of protection from Nazi persecution. She spoke about the proximity of the Russians, and expressed her desire that they quickly liberate her area, which was filled with concentration camps.

Caroline finished her soup and whispered her thanks to Mitzi. Mitzi told her she would send again for the doctor the next day, so she bade Caroline good night. Caroline could not remember the last time she had had a meal of any kind, let alone one served with such kindness. If she possessed the energy, she might have been able to cry with gratitude. But as it was, she fell into a deep sleep, relishing the delicious comfort of her soft bed and the kindness of her saviors. When the doctor came the next day, he suggested that Caroline be admitted to the hospital. She had contracted typhus and severe pneumonia, and her condition was very serious. The doctor informed them that the Allied troops were taking over the area. As soon as that happened, he would make the necessary arrangements to have her hospitalized. In the meantime, he prescribed her with antibiotics to help her survive until she could be transferred to a hospital.

Over the next few weeks, Caroline slowly regained her strength; she gained some weight and even managed to take a shower, as long as Mitzi held her arms. She was always expressing her gratitude to Mitzi for her clean, fresh clothing, a welcome change from the filthy, lice-infested clothing she had been forced to wear at the camp. To Mitzi, it was a joy to learn that such simple comforts, such as fresh linen and hot soup, could bring Caroline pleasure. The two women became firm friends.

One afternoon, Mitzi asked Caroline if she would like to tell her a little about herself. Aware that Caroline had endured some horrific experiences, Mitzi had been careful not to bring up anything that might be a source of pain to this poor young woman. She had bided her time for weeks before asking Caroline to open up to her. Caroline told her about her childhood in Rotterdam, her marriage to Soli, and her separation from her baby; she was surprised at the ease with which she could open her heart to Mitzi. But when she began to talk about Auschwitz, she thought about Eva for the first time, and broke down in tears. It was Eva who had stood by her through the lowest points in her life, and she could not bear the thought of Eva enduring yet more pain.

"*Arme, arme schatselle*," whispered Mitzi, when Caroline could no longer speak from her sorrow. "Poor, poor dear! When Fritz first found you in the snow, half dead, he burned your striped clothes as soon as he could. He was terrified some passing Nazi guard would see it and suspect that someone was harboring a Jew. We took you into the barn to disinfect you because we didn't want any lice to come with you into the house. Poor girl! You were so vulnerable and weak! We were lucky you had no hair on your head so we could make sure we'd removed the lice entirely!"

Caroline laughed softly, and found herself unconsciously moving her hand up to her head to feel the new little hairs growing there. Mitzi smiled.

"You are beginning to look very feminine again," she said. Caroline looked at the tattoo engraved on her arm for eternity, and asked, "How could you and Fritz take such risks? By taking me in, you are putting yourselves in danger. Anyone can see I've 'escaped' from a camp. Aren't you afraid you will be caught? You stand to lose everything."

"Well, it is a long story," sighed Mitzi, "but perhaps it will help you understand if I explain the following. Let me fill you in on the history of the nearby Mauthausen concentration camp. As early as August 8, 1938, a few months after the *Anschluss,* the first prisoners were transferred to the new concentration camp. The camp was established to house political prisoners who opposed the Nazis, including members of the clergy who preached against Nazi ideology. Prisoners of the camp were forced to work in the Mauthausen quarry to extract the materials for the magnificent building projects in Linz. Before the construction of the first Gusen Camp, the prisoners of Mauthausen concentration camp in Austria had to march some four kilometers [almost two and a half miles] every day to reach the stone quarries at Gusen. When the Gusen sub-camp was opened in 1940, prisoners who worked the quarries were housed there. The guards were excessively brutal with their prisoners, who were killed quickly, as a result of the abuse.

"With the capture of Poland by the Nazis, the camps were again repopulated with new prisoners. Soon, Gusen ii and iii were opened subterraneously as camps that would produce weaponry. The deadly work at these camps was carried out by Hungarian and Polish Jews. These camps were classified as Level Three Camps.

"This designation indicated that all the camps' prisoners would be terminated at the camp. The Gusen camps were among the least known of all Nazi concentration and work camps. This is not because they were among the smallest camps – these camps housed what were probably the largest numbers of prisoners – but simply because most prisoners did not survive to tell the tale."

Mitzi paused to sip some water and continued:

"We were devout Catholics who attended church in the diocese in Linz. In 1938, the Nazi Party started to crack down on the clergy and arrested many priests who spoke out against them. These priests were among those imprisoned in the concentration camp. When Dr. Johann Gruber, our priest, was arrested for his outspoken views against the Nazi annexation of Austria, all of us were up in arms about what would happen to others who shared his beliefs. As fate would have it, he was transferred to the nearby KZ Gusen camp at Langenstein. As more and more priests were taken away, the hostility towards the Nazis grew within our devout Christian community. To make matters worse, we had all seen pictures of the Nazis wrecking beautiful, famous churches in Poland and openly committing sacrilege.

"In 1940, when the Vatican managed to cajole the Nazis into improving conditions for the imprisoned priests, most of the clergy were transferred to much milder work camps. But our Dr. Gruber volunteered to remain in that most horrible KZ Gusen camp, so that he could help hundreds of Polish and Spanish comrades to survive. As Dr. Gruber had been well connected in Austria, the SS granted him special privileges, which he often used to help his comrades in the camp. A real 'break' came when the railway construction project was interrupted by the discovery of an ancient Bronze-age burial ground. Dr. Gruber was allowed to lead the archeological dig on the site, and as a reward for his work, he was granted some 'extra' privileges. This heralded the beginning of 'Gruber's Organization,' a resistance group born in one of the most brutal concentration camps. At that time, we became involved in the clandestine movement of resistance against the Nazis.

"As part of his duties, Dr. Gruber was allowed to maintain contact with people outside the camp. He regularly spoke to archeologists and other support people from the museums and universities. He was able to raise funds from friends and supporters on the outside, which were smuggled into the camp. At the same time, he arranged for archeological findings to be registered in museums outside the camp. With the funds, he would bribe SS officers and kapos, so that he could organize food distribution within the camp and ensure that the starving prisoners were fed. In this way, he was able to save many a poor soul from death.

"We were asked by members of the Gruber Organization to supply milk and eggs, which were to be smuggled into the camp by paid collaborators. Eventually, we were asked to hide an escaped prisoner, who had been shot by the SS. In the end, we were able to help this prisoner leak information about KZ Gusen out of the camp.

"The first reports were shocking. They consisted of brutal accounts of the extermination of inmates, and priests in particular. The lowest ranking group of prisoners, the priests were often treated the most cruelly. Even religious practice was forbidden in the camp, and several hundred priests were killed after being betrayed by other inmates, who were anxious to avoid their own punishments. The camp commander, Jentzsch, devised his own method for killing the priests: he would wait until they returned from their hard labor in the stone quarry, and sent them exhausted and starving into freezing cold showers. They were forced to remain in the icy water until they died, which, in these conditions, would often take place in less than thirty minutes. Over the course of three months, Jentzsch murdered sixty inmates, forty-one of them priests. Jentzsch delighted in his nickname 'Bademeister,' which meant 'bath attendant.' For him, it was a kind of acknowledgment for his work.

"Gruber continued to tell us that the filthiest and most exhausting tasks were always reserved for the Jewish inmates. Their average length of survival at the camp was two weeks. These first reports caused a tremendous stir among the members of our church and the friends and acquaintances of Dr. Gruber. These persecutions defied everything the Bible stands for, but unfortunately there was not much we could do to stop it," Mitzi concluded.

Fritz entered the room, and stood silently, listening to his wife speak.

Finally, he said, "It was the second report that really shocked everyone," forcing their attention toward him. "While working at the camp, Dr. Gruber wrote a detailed report, denouncing medical experiments conducted at the KZ Gusen camp. It was from this report that we learned the Nazis intended to create a pathology museum in the camp's Block 27. They planned to create specimens for the museum by executing *en masse* all those inmates who were ill. They killed their victims by administering lethal injections in the region of the heart. The goal was to obtain 286 specimens of human organs and keep them on display at the museum. Other activities in the museum included biological experimentation of different diseases, including one conducted by Dr. Helmut Vetter. He experimented with tuberculosis and used the inmates as unwilling guinea pigs for his 'Ruthenol' trials. Dr. Gruber pleaded with the superiors in the church to expose all of these activities to the International Red Cross and the world press."

"So you see," continued Mitzi, "these barbaric actions compelled us to act against the Nazis, to do whatever we could to stop them. We saved four inmates by sheltering them here until other people in our group could find a way to transfer them elsewhere. Now that the Germans are losing ground, all we can do is wait…."

Fritz interjected, "Auschwitz was liberated by the Russians over two weeks ago!"

"Are they liberating this area as well?" Caroline asked.

"I should hope so," said Fritz. "The Allied Forces are close by, and are bombing every day; our sources tell us that in a few weeks they will take over. Germany is collapsing and the Fuehrer himself is surrounded by the Soviet Army."

"And how is Dr. Gruber doing?" Caroline asked.

"Someone betrayed the organization," said Mitzi sadly. She described how Dr. Gruber had been tortured horribly for three days the previous April, and how he eventually succumbed to death on Good Friday. Dr. Gruber died a painful silent death, not uttering one word of information about his colleagues. After his death, many inmates were denied the food that Gruber had once distributed to them.

"As soon as Dr. Gruber was caught," continued Mitzi, "all the other priests in the concentration camps were stripped of their administrative positions. But our organization is still very active and we have our 'eyes' in the camps…."

Caroline had become very tired from this lengthy conversation with her hosts, so she excused herself and returned to her room to rest. So much information, such kindness – it was imperative that she recover. Now that the war was ending, and she saw how her own people had fought bitterly against her oppressors, she felt that she could find the strength to restore her faith. All she wanted, at this moment, however, was to sleep.

During the next few months, the Allied forces bombed the Gusen camps. The local resistance pinpointed the targets and transmitted their precious news to the British bomber, who dropped their fiery cargo on all the right spots.

Caroline had gained a few pounds, but she was still very weak. Her only chance of survival was to be admitted to a hospital, where she could receive proper medical care. One Sunday morning, Fritz told the women that a Red Cross representative from Switzerland was on his way to their home to talk to them about their experiences in the war. It seemed too good to be true, but outsiders were beginning to arrive, and they were looking for evidence of Nazi brutality. Caroline was happy to oblige such a request, if only she could get out of bed and get dressed to meet the visitor.

Louis Haefliger, from Switzerland, was part of a Red Cross mission that had arrived in trucks filled with food for the camp prisoners. He was shocked to discover that he would be barred entry into the camp. When this happened, he returned with his trucks to St. Georgen-Gusen and met with local members of the Resistance. This is how he and Fritz met. Fritz invited him back to meet his wife and Caroline. During his visit, Fritz and Mitzi revealed the reality of life at the Mauthausen and Gusen camps. Fritz told him that the Germans were planning a mass extermination by blasting the underground installations and killing the inmates, and most likely many local residents, as well. Then Caroline told him a little bit about events at Auschwitz, and her experience with Dr. Mengele in particular. After hearing such shocking accounts, Louis realized that far more needed to be done than simply distributing food to the camp prisoners; he had to actively prevent the upcoming destruction. Louis returned to the KZ Mauthausen central camp on April 30, 1945, and was provided accommodation by Ostuf Reimer, the chief of counter intelligence at Mauthausen. Reimer, like Louis, was a bank clerk in civilian life, and the two built a good rapport. Reimer confirmed the Germans' secret plans of mass extermination. Louis violated the Red Cross rules, and brought in Allied troops to liberate the camps.

On May 6, Caroline was awakened by Mitzi, who wanted her to hear the fantastic news that Fritz had just come home to share with them. The house reverberated with excitement as several neighbors had come in to join them.

Fritz began, "It all started yesterday morning when Louis Haefliger, from the Red Cross, picked me up in an SS car that had been converted into a Red Cross vehicle, which he had obtained with Reimer's help. They had painted it white, and a Red Cross flag replaced the Nazi one. They needed me to guide them to the valley of the Gusen River, north of St. Georgen, where the Americans were stationed...."

Chapter 17
Liberation Nears

O N THE FEAST of Saint Lambertus, the patron saint of Veghel, the skies resounded with the whirring noise that heralded the end of the war. Tilly held Jantje as they came out of church, smiling up at the blue sky and the warm sun.

"Look, Jantje," she laughed, as the baby in her arms stared upwards, "soon it will be over!"

He gave her a big smile and she hugged and kissed him. She was so overjoyed that at last, the end was near. Bertie and Susanne followed Tilly and Jantje back to the hotel, where it was time to start preparing lunch. The streets were filled with excited people, who rushed out of their homes to see the air fleet as it flew overhead. Aircrafts droned loudly while the sky itself was filled with the billowing mushroom forms of hundreds of parachutes. The dazzling parachute silks opened one by one as each parachutist floated slowly to the ground below. As they drew closer to the land, the rainbow of colors of their uniforms and cargo became increasingly real. These messengers of God brought with them cargo and ammunition, brightly colored scooters, guns, anything they could use to rid Veghel of the last of the Nazi soldiers. This was the largest air landing ever seen in Veghel, and to its inhabitants, it signalled only one thing – liberation. Veghel readied itself to meet the troops, gathering in the streets to welcome their saviors. They were filled with a fiery optimism that came from finally being able to act against their oppressors.

Young men eager to fight ran out to meet the soldiers and stood guard over the bridges in the town. From that moment on, everyone knew deep in their souls that no Nazi would ever harm one of the ancient bridges again.

The German soldiers in Veghel fled in terror, and one opened fire, killing a girl who had spent months in hiding in Veghel. They could see the huge army approaching. Tilly's patrons hurried through their lunches, and rushed out of the hotel to watch as this miracle manifested itself. From the terrace of the hotel, Bertie and Lia watched hundreds of c-47 planes fly just barely over their heads, like a mass of birds soaring directly toward its destination. Meanwhile, the enemy scurried away, hoping to find cover, but instead encountered heavy resistance from the townspeople. For four years, the people of Veghel had watched their every step, their hearts racing with fear; on this day, they publicly demonstrated their hatred of their cruel oppressors. The Nazis were still a force to be reckoned with, but the townspeople wanted to convey the message to the Nazis that they could no longer instill the fear of death in them.

Bertie felt an eerie sensation when things suddenly grew silent. A loud voice broke the stillness, yelling, "Get inside! The Nazis are coming!"

Hurriedly, Bertie picked up his children and rushed into the hotel, closing the doors loudly behind him. He had just seen a soldier approaching with his gun. Bertie heard the shots of the machine gun as he entered the dark silence of the empty hotel.

"To the cellar!" ordered Bertie, as the bullets began to fly. The staff fell to the floor to dodge the shots, and the whistling noises caused everyone's hair to stand on end. Susanne quickly took the children underground, and reluctantly left Bertie while he and the staff lay on the floor. He waved a number of the hotel guests down the stairs with her. Bertie made his way to the window to take a look outside, but all he could see were four German soldiers retreating, as the gun shots grew louder and louder.

Suddenly the windows of the hotel shattered. Bertie fell to the floor in terror. He didn't hear anyone come into the hotel, and was surprised to feel the end of a gun on his shoulder as he crouched under the window.

"How do we get upstairs?" shouted the Nazi. Bertie slowly got up and led them to the staircase. At the top of the stairs, he pushed open the door, while another soldier hurried along behind them. They pushed him aside as they found a window facing the street and quickly forgot all about him as they focused on the Americans below. Bertie ducked the plaster and glass that came flying in from the street. Forgotten by the soldiers, Bertie made his way back downstairs to the safety of the ground floor. As he stepped onto solid ground, there was an explosion above him, followed by complete silence. Bertie strained his ears to hear if he could detect quick scurrying or shouts, or even gunfire. He listened for several minutes, but still could not hear anything. A thin plume of smoke and the scent of gunpowder made its way under the closed door. He did not know how he could be so sure, but he realized that the soldiers in his room were dead. He climbed the stairs again and found them lying in a pool of blood. He closed the door, then went downstairs to the basement to find his wife. The survivors bombarded him with a barrage of questions.

Two hours later, Bertie heard stomping footsteps above his head, and when he opened the cellar door he was greeted by an arched array of machine guns. The little American flags he saw on the soldier's uniform told him he was dealing with Americans now, but he could sense the Americans had no idea what to do with him. The man who appeared to be their leader fixed his gaze on Bertie, and drew himself up stiffly. Bertie cleared his throat.

"Don't shoot, please, don't shoot," he said, trying to sound as calm as possible, using the little English he knew. "I am a Hollander and the owner of this hotel!"

"OK, bud," answered the sergeant. "Where are the Krauts?" he asked loudly.

The American had not shifted his position, and his gun was still pointed at Bertie. It took a while for Bertie to realize what it was that the American wanted from him, but when he finally understood, he tried to respond clearly.

"There are two of them upstairs," he said finally. "I think they are dead from a grenade."

"Any Germans in your cellar?" asked the sergeant.

"No sir, just my wife and two children. Some hotel guests and staff…we have been hiding there for the last two hours."

"OK," said the soldier, softening his stance. "Go back downstairs, till we check out the place," said the American. He turned to the soldiers around him and ordered, "Willy, go down with him and see that everything is OK."

Half an hour later, the bar was filled with at least a dozen American soldiers. Bertie was finally able to put the sergeant at ease by talking to him calmly, and offering hospitality to the Americans. As long as the cold beer flowed and Susanne's food kept on coming, the soldiers were happy in the hotel.

On the other side of Veghel, in Sluisweg, where soldiers were parachuting out of aircrafts, Gijs Bossert could see the different colored smoke bombs being lit around him as the liberating army set up camp. He watched as the soldiers split up into groups and reported to their superiors in their different units.

Gijs approached one of these soldiers to introduce himself as a member of the Dutch Underground, and followed the soldier for an introduction to an officer. The soldier nodded, then immediately introduced Gijs to Col. Howard R. Johnson, the commanding officer of the 501st Regiment of the 101st Division. Gijs immediately set to work detailing information that he and his brother Ko had gathered and worked with during the war. From the outset of the invasion, the Dutch Underground had established contact with the 101st Division. Now that the division had finally arrived, the men were able to work together, in person, signifying an historical moment. They pored over the maps and plans together for the first time as a group. For years, they had worked together as strangers, the unknown Americans assisting the Dutch resistance soldiers; now they were finally able to put a face to a name.

They would work together now to seize the bridges leading into Veghel. Colonel Johnson and Gijs went over the goals of their mission. The 501st Division would land in the vicinity of Eerde and Veghel and seize four key bridges. Two were to be highway bridges and the others were railroad spans. They were also to hold a specific segment of the road. The 502nd Division would seize bridges over the Dommel River at St. Oedenrode, while another division would move to Best to capture the highway bridge, south of the town. The 506th Division would take the bridge over the Wilhelmina Canal at Son, and continue south to Rindhoven, where they would meet the British army moving north.

"Today," announced Colonel Johnson with no small amount of pride, "marks the beginning of the liberation of South Holland."

Word had now reached the Americans that there had been a small hitch in their plans, as Lt. Colonel Harry Kinnard and his 1st batallion of the 501st had passed landing zone A and had landed on the grounds of Heeswijk Castle, about five miles north of Veghel. Kinnard left some men behind in the castle, which they had occupied, and made his way to Veghel where he took over the defenseless bridge over the Aa River and started to crack down on German resistance in Veghel. Gijs and Ko Bossert had brought Johnson up to date on the underground movement and its contacts. Already, many young men from Veghel, who had helped the resistance during the war, were cleaning the streets of unwanted elements. They proudly wore their orange arm bands, which signified their involvement with the Resistance. Another member of the KP, Ton Kuyper, left in the morning, with orders to clean up Hertogenbosch. Once his mission was accomplished, he returned to the Hoogstraat Number 8, the house of the Kerssemakers, which temporarily served as the regiment's headquarters. He looked like he had been through a battle. He found Gijs and the rest of the group with Colonel Johnson.

"So, what happened?" queried Gijs.

"It was a nightmare, but I was lucky," he responded, giving the following report. "I was on the way back here, when I was stopped by a German soldier near Coudewater, who demanded that I give him my bike. He tried to take it off me, but I had a pistol and armbands in the bag, which was attached to the bike. I asked if I may take the bag, as my clothes were inside. The German agreed. Thank God, he did not check the bag! I walked over to the infirmary of Coudewater, and was supplied with a bike. Reaching Heeswijk, where the Americans had landed at the castle, I decided to join them. I went to the castle to report and clarify the situation. In the inner yard lay a bunch of wounded Americans. They asked me from which direction the Germans would come. But we did not take into account that they could be coming from the direction of Zuid-Willemsvaart. I went back out and joined the soldiers at the corner in the S curve, where we waited for the Germans. At about 16:00 hours, the first two Germans arrived in a motorcycle with a side-car. We opened fire and they skidded off the road, and we took them as prisoners. A few minutes later, another car came along, which we fired at as well. All the occupants were killed. A little later, a Red Cross truck appeared with four German soldiers inside.

"We forced it to stop. They asked permission to pass, because it was a Red Cross truck, but I told the Americans, 'Don't count on it, lately we don't see anything but Red Cross wagons, and they are all full of weapons.' The Germans had to empty all the contents out of the truck on the road, and of course, there were a lot of arms.

"I said, 'We are going with this Red Cross wagon to the hospital in Veghel with our wounded.'

"We had the first two wounded soldiers lying in the truck when the Germans appeared from the Aa River. All I could do was run and jump into a ditch along the main highway, and wait. There also lay several Americans. After about a half an hour, an American who was lying next to me was killed. I waited until 20:00 hours, and made my way here by foot!"

Johnson complimented Ton on his relentless efforts, and asked him if he was strong enough to continue working with them that night. Gijs was to lead a patrol of six men to the bridge over the Zuid-Willemsvaart, and they headed out in the direction of Eerde. When they arrived, he acquired a 9 mm revolver from the arms cache.

In order to get to the bridge as quickly as possible, the men rode on bikes. The bridge was to be the strategic point between Eindhoven and Nijmegen. Before they left, they lit a smoke signal for the troops behind them, signalling that they had installed a machine gun post for their use. Then the patrol went on ahead to Veghel, where Gijs proceeded to caution all villagers to remain indoors. There were approximately one hundred armed Germans patrolling the area where Gijs was to work. He was aware of their presence and prepared himself as he moved within their range. Inevitably, he knew that he would be targeted. By the bridge over the Aa River, near City Hall in Veghel, gunfire suddenly came from the direction of the market. Gijs and his men took refuge behind the bridge wall and returned fire. While he was fighting, Gijs was informed by a parachutist from behind the bridge that he should go directly to Colonel Johnson, who had reached the bridge over the Zuid-Willemsvaart.

Gijs started on the long trek toward the Colonel. He crawled past the Kuyper family's bicycle store to the dry moat near the Kerssemakers' house. Bullets zoomed past his ears as he surfaced from the moat, but in his amazement, he saw no one except an American soldier, shooting at him from a nearby elm.

Gijs dropped to the ground, and screamed in fury, "I am a member of the Dutch Underground," then muttered under his breath, "You oaf!"

His heart was pounding so hard that he was sure that every German in the vicinity could hear him.

"Sorry," yelled the American. "You're lucky. That's the first time I've ever missed."

Once again, Gijs and Johnson set out to revise the maps and coordinate communication with troops entering Veghel. While they worked, they watched a bus approach along the canal. As it passed, the soldiers and Gijs took cover, and shot at the bus, sending the loaded vehicle swerving off the road and into the ditch. The bus was full of German soldiers and a number of Nazi youths, many of whom were seriously injured in the crash. When they returned to Veghel, they learned that twenty-eight Germans had been killed and fifty had been taken prisoner; the rest had fled. But no one was deluded into believing that their work was done. For the next few days, all the Underground soldiers, as well as the American troops, anticipated danger lurking in every quiet corner.

Colonel Johnson took over the home of Dr. Kerssemakers, converting it into the regimental headquarters. From that point on, everyone in the town worked together to aid the Americans in their battle against the Nazis. Complying to the request of Gijs Bossert and his comrades, the farmers brought their carts into the yard of the headquarters, filled with all the parachutists' equipment, originally left behind in the landing fields. The big battles were still to come, and the whole town prepared in earnest.

Soon it became apparent that not all the American troops would be able to make it to Veghel, and that changes would need to be made to the town's roads and bridges to allow for foreign vehicles to access Col. Johnson's regiment. Gijs and the other resistance fighters rallied together and pooled all of the town's resources to solve this problem. Two of the American soldiers' platoons would work on the construction and widening project for the Zuid-Willemsvaart bridge, but materials and human resources were needed to complete the monumental task. Ton Kuyper was ordered to gather the people together, and explain to them the meaning and importance of this task. He visited the director of the technical school, and within a short period of time, he had enlisted a group of teachers ready to work on the bridge project. Huge iron balls, wood and fastening materials had to be gathered and transported to the site before morning, so that work could begin. All through the night, the material arrived. Wood was sawn, and nine iron balls were retrieved from Kuyper's yard. By 5:00 A.M., on September 19, Ton and several dozen helpers were at the bridge ready for the army engineers.

The people of Veghel were deliriously happy at the prospect of being liberated. They embraced each other, shook hands, and danced in the streets. Liters of beer and canned milk were served, and the women prepared countless baskets of fruit for the Allied troops who streamed into the town. The Dutch couldn't do enough to show the Americans their appreciation. But the Nazis were not yet ready to relinquish their control over the small town, and so the German counterattack began.

Chapter 18
The Liberation of Mauthausen and Gusen

May 5, 1945

PLATOON LEADER, Sgt. Albert J. Kosiek, of the First Platoon of Troop D, 41st Cavalry Reconnaissance Squadron, Mechanized of 11th Armored Division, 3rd U.S. Army, started out early from the town of Katsdorf, about two miles north of the Gusen camp. His mission was to examine the bridges at St. Georgen and ensure that they were intact. As they were located on a route used by Nazi forces, he suspected that the bridges had been sabotaged in anticipation of his arrival. The platoon came in via the mountainous Müehlviertel Region to avoid the heavy fighting at Linz. As Sgt. Kosiek advanced with his platoon, they encountered a makeshift roadblock – a pile of logs placed squarely in the middle of the road. They got out and checked it gingerly for any trip wires or booby traps.

In the distance, a motorcycle that was leading what appeared to be a Red Cross vehicle approached them on the road. The driver waved a white flag as he slowly moved towards the officers. The Americans stood and aimed their guns. Fritz, and his friend Louis Haefliger, who worked with the Red Cross, emerged from the white car to face dozens of Americans pointing their guns. They knew the Americans were not taking any chances.

Reimer, who was riding the motorcycle in front of them, dismounted and raised his arms to face the troops. Louis and Fritz followed suit. The Americans checked them for arms, and once they were satisfied, they brought the three men to their platoon leader, Sgt. Kosiek.

In broken English, Fritz attempted to communicate with the Americans, until a Jewish man named Rosenthal, who spoke German, stepped forward. Louis breathed a sigh of relief at having found a common language, and slowly told Rosenthal the details. Fritz explained that he and Louis were Red Cross delegates, whose mission it was to plead with the Americans to liberate the Gusen and Mauthausen concentration camps. Fritz informed the Americans about the number of SS guards at the camps, and led them to believe that the guards would surrender. The Americans agreed to cooperate, as long as a constant radio connection be maintained during the effort. Kosiek then joined the three men in their vehicles, and instructed Fritz to lead the troops in the white car. On the way, they encountered many German soldiers who readily surrendered.

On the way, they stopped at the Gusen camp where the SS captain in charge willingly surrendered, and was told that they would be picked up on the way back from Mauthausen. He insisted that they keep their weapons because he feared that they would not be able to keep order in the camp otherwise, and prevent the inmates from taking revenge and killing them.

As they left, the German guards gave them an American salute. As they continued, they reached Mauthausen, which was located at an altitude, and was flanked on one side by the Danube.

Mauthausen was surrounded by enormous cement walls, and the officers were armed with large field cannons, but the SS in charge of defending the area had fled several days earlier. On the other side of the woods was the first entrance to the camp. They stopped the car and got out. This section of the camp was surrounded by an electric fence that was charged with two thousand volts of electricity, but behind the fence were hundreds of people who were wild with joy at the sight of the small group of men. Some prisoners had only blankets to cover themselves, and others stood there completely nude in the cold. At the sight of Reimer, the guard opened the gate. The prisoners surrounded the men as they entered the camp and clamored to touch the American soldiers who had finally come to liberate them.

Kosiek and his men were aghast when they came face to face with the indisputable evidence of brutality and ruthlessness. The sight was so disturbing that several of Kosiek's men ran to the surrounding bushes to vomit. A young English-speaking German, accompanied by the camp commander, told Kosiek that he had ordered all his guards, close to a thousand in number, to surrender. Kosiek and the men proceeded unimpeded to the main section of the camp, where again they were overwhelmed by the raucous cries and shouts of happiness coming from the prisoners. They were greeted by the most spectacular ovation they had ever witnessed. To the prisoners, the arrival of the American soldiers symbolized freedom from torture and horror. Kosiek felt like a celebrity, and was happy that he had cooperated with Fritz in his plan to liberate the camps.

Suddenly, a prisoner stepped forward and introduced himself as Captain Jack Taylor of the United States Navy. He held up his dog tag to Kosiek to prove it. He informed the sergeant that there were two more Americans in the camp and one English pilot in the hospital.

Above the gate was a platform overlooking the courtyard. On the side of the platform were the flags of the thirty-one nations represented in the camp. An International Prisoners' Committee had been established several days earlier, and an English-speaking representative from each country or group was appointed in the camp. They agreed to keep their people in their quarters while Kosiek and his men cleared the camp of the German guards. Then the camp would be in command of the United States Army.

Some of the refugees set up a band in the courtyard. The representatives then spoke, and the first one from Poland called for three cheers for the Americans; the response was thunderous. The band played the Star Spangled Banner, which evoked so much emotion that everyone cried, prisoners and American soldiers in unison. Later it was learned that just the night before, Captain Jack had taught the band the American national anthem.

After inspecting the camp, the Americans were fully aware, for the first time, of the extent of Nazi brutality and torture. Next to the crematorium lay piles of dead bodies that had been left to rot and were torn apart by rats and vermin. For the most part, the bodies did not have any human characteristics. The Americans were shown where the prisoners had been gassed and were told of the process by which bodies were added to the growing heaps outside the crematorium. They were told how the German officers had shown the American prisoners "respect" by shooting them instead of killing them by gas or other means.

They learned of the lies that had been told to the women and children so that they would go willingly to their deaths in the chambers. Fritz shuddered; in all his life, he had never seen so many corpses. Kosiek heard over and over again the countless stories of cruelty and despair from prisoner after prisoner.

The prisoners who had managed, by some miracle, to dodge death consisted of skin and bones. They told Kosiek that the prisoners had been allotted one loaf of bread a week for seven people. The sergeant learned from an eight-year-old Polish boy that if he did not take his hat off and stand to attention when a guard passed by, he would be shot. Other prisoners verified this story and said that many people had been shot because they refused to honor the Germans in this way. With the help of Captain Jack and the other two American prisoners, Kosiek and his men rounded up all of the guards, ordered them to relinquish their weapons, and led them to Gallneukirchen, where the u.s. Army was based. Kosiek radioed headquarters that he was bringing in 1,800 German prisoners, and wanted to know what he should do with them.

Following the liberation of Mauthausen, an armored car and jeep continued on to the Gusen Camp, where they encountered even more horrible sights. Riots had broken out and many prisoners had joined together to lynch their kapos. Finally, the Americans took control of the situation, not yet understanding the cause of the violence and rage in the prison population.

Over forty thousand prisoners from Mauthausen and Gusen were liberated by the Americans, and Louis and Fritz were honored to have been part of such an endeavor.

Back at Fritz's house, Caroline rejoiced at the news, even though she was still so sick from her own experience at Auschwitz. Louis had promised Fritz that as soon as he could organize a free bed in the hospital, he would personally see to it that Caroline would receive proper medical attention. For now, she needed to get back into bed and rest after the latest developments. As soon as Caroline's head hit the pillow, she fell fast asleep. In her dreams, she was happily holding her baby in her arms.

Chapter 19
The Final Battle

JACK THE COOK was a British airman who found himself at the Golden Lion by luck. His plane, shot down during an air maneuver in the area, had crashed in a field close to the hotel. Tilly had found him, nursed him back to health, and put him to work in the kitchen. But she had other plans for him, which involved resistance work, and in this capacity she knew he would be extremely useful. She quickly found a new identity for him, and he officially became "Piet Hein," assuming the identity of a dead citizen, close to Jack's own age. Tilly cut and pasted Jack's weathered photo in Piet's documentation, so that no one would think twice about the validity of his ID, should it be inspected.

Once his identity was in place, Tilly had no problem finding an inconspicuous occupation for Jack, who loved to cook. While he recuperated from his injuries in the Fox's home, he would often concoct some experimental but delicious meals for the whole family. Jack was glad to be able to show his gratitude to the Fox family in a tangible way, doing what he was good at – cooking. Bertie and Susanne easily agreed that Jack would be perfect for the job as chef in their hotel, so Jack eagerly took his place in the family business, working for hours over the hot stoves and ovens, watching over the precious Jantje as he worked. Jack spent hours perfecting the food he prepared. He searched the town for ingredients, and when he could not get what he needed, he displayed creativity in his improvisational skills. But today, Jack set his mind to the task of baking a sumptuous lemon crème birthday cake for the platoon sergeant of the 101st Regiment, but for this occasion, none of his ingenious substitutions would do. He would need the freshest cream and eggs from the farm and newly ground soft flour from the finest grains. It would be difficult to get his hands on lemons, but he contented himself with the knowledge that a small amount of juice and a bit of peel would suffice.

He searched for fruit that would just be ripening, some small, fragrant berries still growing undisturbed in one of the unmolested bushes around the hotel, or perhaps a scavenger hunt through the wooded areas close by would be called for. In Jack's mind, this celebratory dessert deserved the best ingredients. After the fruit had been gathered, and the cream was whisked to a sweetened lightness, he and Jantje would indulge in the extra fruit coulis and cream. He could already imagine the joyous laughter he and the boy would share, licking the batter from the mixing bowl.

Jack had a son in England, named Arthur, who was approximately Jantje's age. His son was constantly in his thoughts, and Jack counted the days till he could be reunited with Arthur once more. He knew, though, that he had to focus his efforts on getting through the war, before returning back to his family and life. When Jack looked at Jantje, he saw the face of his son, Arthur, and lavished fatherly attention on the boy; in turn, Jantje had found a new friend to play with. Jack and Jantje were inseparable in the kitchen, and when the quiet afternoon time approached each day, Jack loved to take Jantje out for a walk in his carriage. He would spend the entire afternoon with Jantje, playing on the swings in the park, and amusing the child with games and songs.

Jantje was so attached to his friend that he would follow him with his eyes whenever he left the room, and would cry if he left him.

Although Jack genuinely enjoyed spending time with Jantje, his involvement with the child also lent his new identity a tangible credibility. Who else but a dedicated chef would obsess about his food in this way? Who else but a loving "uncle" would dote on a baby boy, and take such delight in spending time with him? Jack considered himself truly blessed that his life had been spared, and that he was afforded this new identity that enabled him to spend time with this precious little boy, and practice his culinary skills. He also did not lose sight of the bigger picture – fighting the Nazis.

Jack worked enthusiastically in the kitchen, basking in Jantje's presence, and was hopeful that the war would soon be over. It would only be a matter of days until the Nazis would surrender, giving him the freedom to return home to his family. He sang as he worked a string through the cake's cooling sponge, cutting layers out of the baked softness and its rich lemon and vanilla fragrances. Jantje sang along, filling his mouth with dollops of leftover whipped cream from Jack's bowls. When Susanne came into the kitchen to begin the dinner preparations, she found the kitchen alive with their music, and laughed when she saw Jantje covered in the sweet cream.

"Look at you," she cried, "you're up to your ears in it!"

Jantje laughed, and then licked his lips in an effort to remove every bit from his face. Susanne wet a clean dishcloth with warm water and wiped his smiling, sticky face, while he savored the rare confection. She wrapped her arms around him and he squealed his delight. Both Susanne and Jack delighted in making Jantje laugh, and were absorbed in doing so when Bertie came into the kitchen.

"It's not fair," said Bertie. "You are all having fun with my son, while I do all the work!" Susanne and Jack exchanged mock furtive glances before bursting into laughter, then Susanne happily carried Jantje to Bertie. He tossed Jantje into the air, then caught him in his arms. Jantje knew what it was like to fly high into the open air, breathlessly – then find a secure, happy landing in his father's arms.

In the town, everyone's spirits were high. There was not only the birthday party to celebrate, but the knowledge that the war would soon be over. Tilly had been successful in recruiting the staff of the Golden Lion and the townspeople to work together in constructing an additional bridge over the Zuid-Willemsvaart in time for the liberating armies to arrive in their town. Today they would celebrate their hard work and welcome the arrival of the first tanks over their new bridge.

At about 10:00 A.M., the first black Sherman tank stood at the foot of the bridge, poised to cross over into the town. Hundreds of Veghelaars were there to cheer the Americans on and to welcome what they knew would be the beginning of the end of the war. At exactly 10:05 A.M., the tank started its slow progression over the newly completed bridge. When it finally stopped at the other end, the crowd roared; then an entire parade of tanks, followed by many well-stocked trucks, crossed into the town. As the cheers of the townspeople and the music rose around her, Tilly breathed a sigh of relief. Operation "Market-Garden" was right on track. The corridor was officially open, and the British tanks were on their way. The first part of the 101st Division's plan was complete.

While everyone around her revelled in celebrations that would continue for hours, Tilly made preparations, but as the party progressed, she allowed herself to be entertained by a handsome and interested captain. Bertie watched her with a paternal concern as Tilly talked to the captain. He walked over to his wife where she worked busily behind the bar and put his arms around her waist. He gave her a bit of a start, but she smiled at him and let him kiss her left ear.

"What was that for?" she asked him, smiling.

"Oh, nothing," said Bertie, wrapping his arms around her again. "I just thought that since everyone else was having such a good time, I would come by and see what you were up to. Pretty busy in here, isn't it?" Susanne nodded in agreement.

"Yes, I haven't seen anything like this since we had our big opening party, remember? Such a wonderful night!"

"Like no other," he said. "Let's dance."

Bertie took her arm and led her away from the bar towards the crowd of dancing couples. Despite the crowds of people, they still managed to listen to the soft, lovely music in each other's arms. The melodious, romantic music was suddenly disturbed by the unmistakable drone of an approaching aircraft, which grew louder as it approached the town. From the balcony the groups of planes could be seen coming closer, and the sky around them was filled with what looked like bright orange balloons. They appeared to be massive lamps, easily mistaken for fireworks. Tilly and the captain watched as flaming red balls slowly dropped towards the ground, and when the first explosion sounded, they both realized what they were seeing.

"My God," said the captain. "The Germans are bombing Eindhoven!"

He and Tilly went back inside the inn, and the captain ran to ferry his men out of the Golden Lion and back to their posts. Tilly moved everyone into the cellars. The whole town took cover as Col. Johnson officially ordered everyone off the streets by 9:00 P.M. At the end of a long and happy day, filled with celebration, only the Americans and the KP members remained on the streets of Veghel. The town was deserted and silent as the night progressed. By 6:00 A.M. the following day, the fighting had abated somewhat. Cars and tanks sped over the bridge, then throughout the town. The lull in the fighting reassured everyone that the Germans had once again retreated, and the townspeople resumed their defiant stance. Life appeared to be returning to normal, as once again, the townspeople donned their patriotic colors and took to the streets in victory. In the meantime, Tilly dressed in more subdued clothing. She had been summoned to a meeting at headquarters. For the first time in weeks, the *onderduikers* had surfaced from their hiding places and came out to join the thunderous celebrations. They danced and sang along with everyone else, without fear. Young men, thought to have been prisoners of war in Germany, also appeared again, happily reuniting with their friends and family.

Eliens, the city's mayor, triumphantly made an appearance among the revellers and led the townspeople to reclaim City Hall. He made a great show of commanding his staff members to replace the broken windows and to rehang the broken doors on their frames. This time, everyone felt as if the danger had passed, and began to forget the ravages of the war, but the day ended in sadness as Col. Johnson formally declared the removal of all flags and orange decorations from landmarks in the town. Everyone knew that the Nazis would launch another attack.

At one o'clock in the morning, Bertie and Susanne once again found themselves scrambling down to the cellars with their children and guests, as the noise of grenades and gunfire rang through the streets. Col. Johnson met with Gijs and his group and received Underground reports that German troops were at Hertogenbosch, and were approaching Heeswijk and Veghel. After evaluating their options, Col. Johnson decided to attack the German forces. He issued orders to Lieutenant Colonel Kinnard, the commander of the 1st Battalion, to use his whole battalion for an offensive move in the direction of Heeswijk. In the early morning hours of September 22, 1944, Col. Kinnard's troops occupied Schijndel. He managed to convey the message, via the Underground, that civilians should be kept off the streets. He also received additional information regarding the strength of the German troops.

As the day commenced, so did the preparations for a counterattack. Two battalions from the 501st Regiment were ready in Schijndel, and two battalions from the 502nd Regiment were on their way to St. Oedenrode-Schijndel. At around ten o'clock, Col. Johnson began to make his move, accompanied by British tanks, as the tank commander had refused to accompany the troops the night before in darkness. The 2nd Batallion was left behind in Veghel, ready to defend the town, if necessary. Part of the 506th Regiment prepared to move out to Uden, where Johnson wanted them by 11:00 hours. For the moment, there was no danger for the bridges over the Zuid-Willemsvaart and the Aa, as they were both defended. Behind Col. Johnson was Gijs Bossert, accompanying the column on his motorcycle. The tanks splashed mud, and sprayed Gijs black. As they neared Schijndel, an artillery piece mounted on four wheels took aim at Johnson's jeep. Gijs saw them trying to position themselves to fire, but lost confidence after seeing the strength of the forces that passed by. Gijs shouted at them with all his strength, "*Krieg is aus* [The war is over]." They abandoned the artillery piece, threw down their weapons, and approached with their hands above their heads.

In Schijndel, they joined up with the occupying troops. Hundreds of German soldiers were taken prisoner, and about 170 were wounded. Many Germans had also died during the battle, but there was no accurate count at this time. Gijs observed a German officer remove his equipment, smashing it to the floor, while screaming, "*Diese Schweine, sie habben uns nicht erzahlt, das die Amerikanen Panzer haben* [These swine, they did not tell us that the Americans have Panzers]." Word had spread that the Germans had launched a major attack against Veghel. Only a small battalion was left behind. The eight members of the Underground could not be left behind in Schijndel, as it remained defenseless. They were charged with escorting the 250 German prisoners to Veghel, and received as booty various vehicles, including a German kitchen wagon, which contained peeled potatoes, and big chunks of meat.

Everything was evacuated. The wounded Germans were left behind under the supervision of their own medical team. Stretched out flat on his motorcycle, Gijs headed for Veghel. He crossed the bridge under German fire as several houses burned around him, and he rushed over to headquarters to find out the latest news. The citizens of Veghel were surprised at the intensity of the German attack. They hurriedly evacuated the celebrating streets to take cover in cellars; some were even digging trenches in their yards, which was very dangerous. A third huge attack had just been staged by German troops coming from the North. From Hertogenbosch along the Zuid-Willemsvaart, an attack on the rail bridge was being thwarted. Ambulances with wounded travelled back and forth. Blood dripped on the streets. By the bridge at the Sluis, there was a fierce fire, where many people who had been celebrating the day before were now seeing their harbor and all its goods go up in flames. The Germans continued on their way, steadily approaching the town. Behind the milk factory they passed through the plowed area, crossed the road to Uden and appeared at the "Zeven Eikenlaan," a known crossing point near Uden.

The cellar of the Golden Lion was packed. All the local residents had taken refuge at the hotel, and when Bertie informed latecomers that they were completely full, they turned to the convent Motherhouse of the Sisters or to the hospital cellars, just a couple of blocks away. The cellars were crowded and stuffy, with hardly enough ventilation for so many people in such an enclosed space. To make matters worse, with every attack, the residents of the cellar could hear the whistling noise of the grenades and the droning of the mortars, followed by shuddering and groaning walls. After every new attack, sand fell, and the cellar was soon filled with dust and clouds of smoke. Susanne had her hands full; Jantje was crying, sensing the fear of the people around him. He was also very uncomfortable in the now crammed corner. Lia was clinging to her mother's dress, and panicked with every new explosion.

Throughout the commotion, Bertie and Susanne tried to remain level-headed, and instructed their staff members to go up to the rooms to retrieve bedding. They knew their guests would need somewhere to sleep for the night, even if they only managed to sleep in between bombs. Jack reported heavy damage to the roof and second floor – at least 25 percent of the inn had been destroyed. Some people waited for a pause between attacks, and rushed outside, preferring to risk their lives outside than suffocate inside. In the meantime, nightfall set in, and the attack raged on. Veghel was paying the toll of war!

*Family portrait: Susanne
and Bertie Fox with
Lia and "Jan," 1945*

*Postcard image of the
Golden Lion, 1943*

*"Jan" and the cook from
the Golden Lion, 1945*

Chapter 20
Home to Holland

CAROLINE WAS FINALLY transferred to a hospital where she could be treated for her longstanding pneumonia and typhus. The hospital was crowded with patients from the camps, and as soon as she arrived, she was placed in quarantine. Still, she was happy to be able to recover in the company of people who were just like her – survivors of the camps.

Over the next few weeks, Caroline slowly recuperated and regained some weight and strength. The man in the next bed, named Renee, became a close friend. He was a Belgian who had survived the Gusen camp, and had also suffered from typhus and dehydration. At night he would often scream in his sleep, tormented by horrific memories of his imprisonment. Whenever this happened, Caroline would listen to his stories of hardship. He would always tell her about the kindness of Pere Jacques, a Carmelite friar who was forced to work alongside him in the Gusen tunnel, where they worked twelve hours a day, surviving on a mere loaf of bread, and the occasional beating from the kapos. It was thanks to Pere Jacques's spiritual support that Renee survived the ordeal.

"Caroline, you can't imagine what a saint of a man he was. He would visit our barracks in the evening and motivated many to share the little food they could get; he convinced us that liberation was close, and urged us to hold on." Tears rolled down Renee's cheeks as he described how Pere Jacques's warm encouragement had inspired many prisoners to remain strong until liberation.

"Pere Jacques is in this hospital, we came in the same ambulance, but I think that he has tuberculosis and is most likely dead."

Caroline told Renee about Eva, who had also helped to save her from what she knew would have been utter despair. But unlike Renee, she knew nothing of her friend's whereabouts. It had occurred to Caroline that Eva might well have been killed by her ordeal, and this thought always made her silent with grief. She never articulated this thought out loud, afraid that verbalizing it would somehow make it come true. She wanted to forget about that part of her past and concentrated on getting well. On June 2, 1945, Renee informed Caroline that Pere Jacques had passed away. Liberation had come too late to save him. His French comrades organized an official ceremony in his honor on the balcony of the Linz town hall.

One Friday morning, when Caroline was lying in her hospital bed, she was greeted by a handsome young American officer whose kind smile warmed her insides, as he asked her name.

"I'm Rabbi Abraham Levinsky from Detroit, Michigan, in America," he introduced himself, extending his hand. He seemed so strong and confident, with his warm smile and friendly greeting. Caroline smiled weakly as he continued.

"I had heard from Central Command that there were some Jewish patients here, survivors of the camps, and I thought I would visit you before the Sabbath begins."

Caroline watched as he pulled a small parcel out of his bag and unwrapped the contents in front of her. It contained a couple of white candles, a small bottle of red wine, and a roll of bread. He held them out to her, and asked, "Do you know what these are for?"

Caroline blinked at the objects, experiencing a surge of emotion that was so strong that it threatened to engulf her completely. She began to sob so heavily that the rabbi was afraid he had caused her great pain. It was too much for her to see the Sabbath candles and the wine for *Kiddush*. She pictured in her mind her mother lighting the candles every week, and her father reciting the *Kiddush*. She remembered the faces of each of her brothers and sisters, illuminated softly by the burning candles and the warmth of their love for each other. Suddenly she realized how long it had been since she had thought of them all, or had heard their voices in her mind. She had a feeling that they had all been exterminated. She sobbed so loudly that the rabbi paced back and forth uneasily. He could not get her to stop and finally ran to call the doctor. When they returned, Caroline was given a sedative to stop the convulsive sobbing. Rabbi Levinsky was still shaking at the distress he had caused her. The doctor explained to him that these reactions were not at all unusual.

"Your presence has shocked her back into an awareness of the world she came from, and she has to let the pain out. She has been through quite a lot, rabbi," he said.

Renee, still in the next bed, commented to them, "This woman has been through experiment block at Auschwitz and her whole family was murdered. No person can endure such pain, without being severely scarred."

The two men watched as Caroline finally stopped crying, and quietly fell asleep. Mitzi came to visit Caroline every day and kept her informed of how things were going in the world around them.

Now that the camps had been liberated, news of the Nazi atrocities finally began to reach the rest of the world. People everywhere were exposed to the ghostly images in the newsreels, and everyone had become familiar with the horrifying realities of the war in Europe. They cringed at the images of the starving prisoners in their striped suits; they were terrorized by the photos of the mass graves and crematoria at each camp, and filled with disgust and horror at the sight of so many corpses belonging to small children. The truth was finally out, as the Americans and Russians began the long process of punishing those Nazis responsible for implementing the atrocities that were now being publicized worldwide.

Mitzi found an article in the *New York Times*, which she had brought to read out to Caroline, about Josef Mengele, describing how his background and family life influenced his work in eugenics and later his torturous experiments at the camp. The article depicted, in harrowing detail, the cruel and sadistic experiments Dr. Mengele had conducted on his Auschwitz victims.

"Well," said Caroline when Mitzi finished reading, "they did not exaggerate. I would be willing to testify at this murderer's trial anytime!" Caroline then fell silent.

"To change the subject," started Caroline, "do you have any news about your son's whereabouts?" she asked.

"No," replied Mitzi. Caroline already knew he was reported missing in action, and she began to regret her question. The last thing she wanted to do was cause Mitzi any more concern about her son, now that the war was ending and he had still not returned.

"We hope to hear something any day now," said Mitzi softly. "Louis Haefliger is trying to locate him in a Russian prison camp."

Caroline looked at Mitzi and said, "Yes, I am sure they will find him soon. Don't worry...."

A few days later, Caroline was informed that she would be sent home to Holland via an American plane, and the visitor from the Dutch government, who had come to talk to Caroline, had assured her that she would be able to make some inquiries once she returned to Holland. Caroline was overjoyed at the prospect of finding her child, but was also aware of the possibility that he may not have survived. In any case, she tried her best to regain her strength in order to prepare herself for her journey home. Fritz and Mitzi tried their best to keep her spirits up and encouraged her to believe that she would find her son. They brought her gifts of new clothing and shoes, items she would need for her upcoming journey.

"How can I ever repay the two of you?" Caroline asked. "I owe you two my life, and even now you are buying me gifts."

"We want you to have these things, so you will look nice when you go home," Mitzi replied. Caroline marvelled at her good fortune in finding such wonderful, giving friends as Fritz and Mitzi, and held them both closely as she cried with joy.

"Just stay in touch with us, Caroline," said Fritz, "and let us know how you are doing. We have faith that you will find your baby."

After their visit, Caroline accompanied her two good friends to the door. Fritz pushed something into the pocket of her dressing gown, while Mitzi smiled at her husband. "Just something to get you started with," said Fritz to Caroline, as she raised her eyes to him inquisitively. He gave her a peck on the cheek, then wrapped a protective arm around Mitzi, and walked out. Caroline rushed back to her room, and carefully removed the wrapping from the garment. She removed the lid off the shoebox and pulled the shoes out, one at a time. They were beautiful, simple shoes of dark blue leather, chosen to match the pale blue, print cloth of her new dress. She quickly removed her dressing gown, unfolded the dress, and slipped it over her head. Gingerly she stepped into each new shoe, and felt their soft lift supporting her as she walked. It had been years since she had owned anything so fine, and felt strange in them, yet secure. She thought of the dress Soli had bought her when they had got married. Soli remained in her heart eternally, wherever she went, whatever she did.

Caroline ran her hands through her hair in an attempt to smooth the stray locks, and pinched her cheeks to give them a little color. When she finally faced the mirror, the figure staring back at her was not the emaciated victim she was afraid to see. Instead, she saw a healthy and strong woman who had survived despite all odds. She had still retained her looks, too. As she folded her dressing gown, she remembered that Fritz had tucked something inside the pocket; there she found a crisp green bill. It was the first time she had ever seen American money, and the first time she had ever held one hundred American dollars in her hand.

Caroline had never flown in a plane before, and she was so excited about returning home and finding her son that she never gave a thought to the stories about the danger of flying. The American pilot who flew the plane tried to make her feel as comfortable as possible. He invited her to sit next to him in the cockpit, so that he could reassure her. He was very gracious and charming, and made every effort to entertain her. At one point, she caught him admiring her figure, and thought how wonderful it was to feel feminine and desirable again.

When she landed, she was given 25 florin as a gift from the Dutch government, and was driven to the offices of the Jewish Coordination Commission. She walked into an office full of dozens of other Jews, survivors like herself. She gave the woman at the desk her name and was asked to take a seat. While she waited, she listened to the people around her tell their stories. They were tired and frustrated, but harbored the same hopes as she did of finding a loved one. All their stories were as full of suffering and hardship as her own. Finally, after everyone else had detailed their own experiences, one woman sitting near her asked her to tell them all a little bit about her own ordeal. Everyone encouraged Caroline to speak, and after hearing her story, reassured her that she would most certainly be reunited with her baby. Caroline was waiting to meet Bram de Jong, the person everyone in the waiting room already knew. "Thank God we have this organization, the Jewish Coordination Committee to help us. If anyone can get your baby back, it is Bram!" they reassured her.

Caroline thanked them for their kindness, and then asked how the organization functioned.

Abe, a kindly old man in a jacket and sportscap, answered for them all:

"Bram de Jong is the editor of the Jewish newspaper *Le'Ezrath Ha'am*. A religious Jew, he started the JCC with his wife and friends Ies and Mirjam Spangenthal. They worked together with other Jews to establish the JCC. The JCC incorporated the ideals of other prominent members of the Jewish community, who worked to provide relief for us. Now that the JCC has received its first donations from the American Jewish Joint Distribution Committee, they have become more independent and can help us survivors even more."

Just then, the secretary called Caroline and ushered her into the boardroom, where she met Bram de Jong, Hilda Verwey, Mr. Sternfeld, and Ies Spangenthal.

"Mrs. Kanes," said Bram, "we have not only read your file, but we have begun to try to locate your baby. We found a report filed by the Underground about a baby 'stolen' from a train in Utrecht around the date that you describe. We have spoken to the courier in The Hague who delivered the child to Brabant, and are now checking with the priest who was in charge."

Caroline could not believe what she was hearing. "Is it my baby?" she whispered.

"There is a strong chance that the child delivered to Brabant is yours, but you must be patient, as there is a lot of resistance to the idea of returning children after so many years. That is why Hilda is here with us today, as her organization helps us recover Jewish children."

Caroline looked at Hilda, who cleared her throat and began to speak: "Let me explain who we are and what we are up against. There are very influential groups who combat the return of foster children to their own parents. They have even presented a bill that has been partially adopted by the government, which states that parents who do not reclaim their children within a specific time period will not be allowed to resume their parental duties. The government will assume that they are out of the country and incapable of providing the parental care that is necessary. They will have to prove themselves fit to be parents before they are allowed to resume their relationships with their children.

"So, foster parents are not obliged to have any contact with biological parents until the government agency rules accordingly. We, however, are in luck, as the courier in The Hague who hid your baby does not support this idea. She saved over fifty Jewish children by finding homes to hide them, and she never lost a single one to the Nazis. She is cooperating with us fully to help us return each and every one of the children back to their birth parents. On the other hand, we don't know what the reaction will be when we approach the adoptive parents in Brabant, who have been raising your baby these last two and a half years. You can imagine how difficult it is for an adoptive mother to relinquish her child."

Caroline began to feel alarm, which must have registered on her face. Hilda tried to be reassuring. "Mrs. Kanes, please give us a chance. We are here to help you get your child back and help you get back on your feet."

"What should I do?" Caroline asked.

"Well, to begin with," Bram answered, "we've found you a room in The Hague near the *mikveh* [Jewish ritual bath], and a possible job at the Scheveningen Woman's Detention Center…if you feel up to guarding these Dutch Nazis. You would be considered a 'safe' parent, one with a good job and a home, which would work in your favor in getting your child back. What do you think?"

Caroline was close to tears. "I don't know how to thank you all for your support and kindness. I will do anything to get my baby back!" she said, and accepted the terms gladly.

Ies Spangenthal spoke next: "Mrs. Kanes, now we have some good news for you. Your brother Isaac Nathan is in a hospital in France, and he will soon be released. He was active with the Maquis and in sabotage missions, blowing up railways. He was wounded, but the bullet was removed, and he is recovering well. We will let him know where to find you when he returns to Holland."

Caroline could no longer control herself after hearing this news. She broke down and cried. "I'm sorry, I'm so embarrassed, and so grateful to you all," she said. "I could not begin to thank you for what you've done…and now to hear that my brother is alive… it is too much."

"Don't worry. We are not surprised!" said Hilda. She sat down next to Caroline and put a protective arm around her. "Caroline, we are your people, survivors just like you. The least we can do is help each other to rebuild our lives. Now here is an envelope for you. Take it. It has vouchers for food, clothing, some of your expenses, and your rent. Just take the train to The Hague. Do you know where the *mikveh* is on the Wagenstraat?"

"Yes, yes, thank you all so very much for everything," Caroline replied, sniffling and drying her eyes. Caroline embraced each person in the room and left for the train station.

Sitting in the train on the way back to The Hague, all kinds of thoughts and feelings surged through Caroline, but she still did not have a grip on her emotions.

Les Nathan (bottom left) with group of Dutch volunteers to the Israeli army, 1948

Chapter 21
South Holland – Free At Last

September 27, 1944

IT WAS SEPTEMBER 27, 1944, and the situation in Veghel during the fighting had turned critical. In the Golden Lion, the mood amongst the people was charged. After several days of constant bombing, rockets still whistled through the air, and with each hit, the hotel's foundation trembled. Veghel suffered interminable days of short, but intense, bouts of fighting, as September dragged its heels. Col. Johnson relocated the KP organization to the city hall of Veghel, as Allied troops continued to stream in. Gijs imparted all reports directly to Johnson, since his English was superior to anyone else's in the organization, and acted as translator.

Sjeff de Groot was still in charge, concerning himself mainly with imprisoning NSB collaborators on a ship in the harbor, which had been converted into a jail, and interrogating them. As the attacks on Veghel continued, de Groot diligently relocated these prisoners from one safe place to another, keeping them and the ship safe from bombs or other means of attack, which were being levelled against the town and any army personnel seen there. In the hotel, Bertie, Tilly, Susanne, and Jack were determined to carry on business as usual, despite the persistent attacks that were going on outside their front door. American troops were arriving all the time, and were welcomed by retaliatory German bombings and snipers that plagued the streets.

Bertie courageously ventured outdoors, only to find the streets deserted; there were no people, no cars, and most of the roofs of the surrounding houses had been partially destroyed. The streets glittered with shards of glass. Walking towards the Hezelaarstraat, Bertie observed trucks lined up along the side of the street, and watched American soldiers go from house to house. He almost stumbled over some bodies that had been shot down, and saw that they belonged to American parachutists. Round the corner, he saw a truck loaded with German prisoners pick up the corpses. They stopped just two doors away from him, and were picking up two bodies that had been hit by a grenade. An English tank drove by, releasing its rockets, and Bertie found himself in the midst of fire. The Germans instantly returned fire and grenades. Bertie ducked, rushing back to the safety of his cellar.

Back at the hotel, he attempted to describe what he had seen to his curious family, staff and guests. The background noise of machine-gun fire and flying rockets told them that they were surrounded by German troops. They prayed fervently that they would not be recaptured.

Gijs arrived at the hotel just in time to partake of the sandwiches that Susanne and Jack had prepared for the evening meal. As soon as he stepped inside, he collapsed in the corner, totally exhausted from the day's activities. His appearance bore witness to the harsh reality of the battle – his face was covered with cuts and bruises, and his leather jacket was caked in mud. Tilly served him hot coffee and sandwiches, which he wasted no time in gulping down.

After Gijs had regained his breath, and satisfied his hunger, he related the latest events; there was a lot to tell. He informed them about the trip he had taken with Lt. Murphy and company to the dunes around Eerde.

"The lieutenant sat on the back of my motorcycle as we followed the jeeps ahead of us. When we reached our destination, we dispersed and entered the dunes. We were combing the dunes when we joined up with another group led by Lt. Fuquay. When we encountered an open area, all hell broke loose, and we ducked for cover. One American soldier named John fearlessly ran with his machine gun to an open space, dropped to the floor, and opened fire on the Germans. He shot so fiercely and effectively that the German defense was crushed. John's heroism must have been contagious, as three fellow soldiers followed suit, opening fire with their machine guns. Before long, the whole section was charging wildly across the open space, which consisted of about 100 meters, attacking the enemy position.

"Mortar fire fell all around us, bullets cut the grass near my feet, but the Americans charged on, shooting all the time. Three parachutists boldly jumped into the Germans' foxholes, and from only a meter or two away, eliminated the enemy. The onslaught was so fierce that the Germans literally did not know what had hit them. There was no time to think, spontaneous action was called for. There was no stopping these indefatigable troops, who, despite being starving and weak, were relentless in their goal to mow down the Germans.

"About forty to fifty Germans fled, leaving behind eighteen dead, along with half a dozen machine guns. We took seven prisoners, who, except for one, were all wounded. We continued to clear the German dunes, even though we were being attacked by mortars from a 60 mm gun. We reached a spot where there was a huge sand hill; between us and the enemy, there was an open area. Murphy, an American soldier, was discussing the next move when an undetected German tank, about 800 meters to our left, opened fire at us. The first salvo killed Lt. Fuquay and one of his sergeants, whose face was blown away from the same explosion.

"Sgt. Kushner, the group leader, was seriously wounded. At that moment, the enemy launched a counterattack, infuriating the Americans so much that they lost all clarity and rationale. There was no more ranking, no officers or leaders; we were united in combat against the Germans, and once more, charged through the dunes, attempting to eliminate the German threat.

"In groups of two and three, soldiers attacked the enemy of their own volition; the Germans now found themselves under attack from all sides.

"I saw three Americans advance rapidly towards a machine-gun nest, and without taking a hit, they eliminated the enemy. The climax came when a third section under Lt. Mier attacked from the right. His men attacked with an indescribable fury, the likes of which I have never seen. The Germans tried to retreat, but were under target from all sides; only a trickle managed to escape. I was in charge of supervising the prisoners, twenty-six in total. We later counted eighty-four dead Germans. We had lost seven soldiers and one officer; the casualties consisted of twenty-three seriously wounded, and ten lightly wounded.

"In the morning, I drove Dan Murphy back to Veghel, when an ammunition truck received a direct hit while passing near Eerde. From the impact, we were thrown off the motorcycle and miraculously landed in one piece several feet away. Where the truck had once stood, there was now a huge crater with many dead and wounded. I managed to reach the church just as the tower that had served as a lookout post came crashing down. Inside there was not a recognizable soul. I heard some noise coming from the cellar. Here I found about forty people reciting the Bible, as the priest lead them in prayer. Some of the children were crying. In the village, there was still more work to be done; there were Germans who were still occupying homes, and I imagined that there was a lot I could achieve with an American parachutist gun, but not having eaten in twenty-four hours, I was ravenous. The stove still burning in the parish kitchen, I grabbed a frying pan, found some butter, and smashed three eggs inside.

"Just then, a grenade landed outside the front door; from the force of the blast, the kitchen door flew off its hinges, leaving ashes. I jumped through the window for safety. The Americans were bringing more troops in, as well as a division of tanks from the British Army. The fighting was bloody everywhere. I witnessed three British tanks being destroyed. I learned from the German prisoners that they belonged to the elite unit of battalion Jungwirth, a parachutist battalion. The Germans were counterattacking with elite units, but now that I have seen these Americans in action, I can tell you, there is no stopping them. It is only a matter of days before they eliminate the Germans."

The occupants of the cellar in the Golden Lion hotel were moved, and relieved, by Gijs's impassioned account; they finally allowed themselves to believe that it was only a matter of time before they would be truly free. Jan and Lia were amusing themselves in the far corner of the cellar, blissfully oblivious to the havoc and destruction that was taking place, just a hundred feet away. Susanne had supplied them with toys that kept them busy and out of mischief.

Ton Kuyper came in, also looking exhausted, and sat down next to Gijs. Two days ago, he had received orders from Colonel Johnson's office to investigate the area around Keldonk. He proceeded on his mission, as instructed, and crossed the bridge. There was not a German in sight. The next morning, he was informed by the Americans that German troops had advanced towards the area in the early hours of the morning, and were digging in between Keldonk and Veghel. He was ordered to continue in his investigations, this time accompanied by a female agent by the name of Nelly Wijnen, as she could nose around without arousing too much suspicion. Their task was to estimate the extent of the damage, and to report back immediately.

Just as they passed the foremost post of the Allies, they spotted a motorcycle lying on the ground that the Germans had left behind. The Americans asked Ton and Nelly if they could bring in the motorcycle, and were about to do this when suddenly machine guns began to fire all around them. Ton dropped the bike and ducked for cover, urging Nelly to do the same. She must not have heard, because she continued walking to the other side of the road, right into the enemy's fire. There was nothing for Ton to do but watch as she fell on the side of the road. Nelly must have been lying there a couple of minutes when Ton heard her cry for help. He shouted to her that he could not come to help her, as it would be suicidal, in the face of German fire. Ton remained where he was, but Nelly's moans and cries increased. He decided to take the risk, and crawled towards her under enemy fire. When he reached Nelly, he saw that she had been shot in the ankle, and was bleeding profusely. Not having any bandages with him, Ton bandaged her foot with Nelly's shawl. Ton's presence calmed Nelly, and she began to relax.

All this took place under heavy machine-gun fire. To escape from this heavy barrage of fire, Ton and Nelly started to crawl on their bellies in the direction of Veghel. As Nelly was exhausted, both emotionally and physically, Ton had to constantly help her. Along the way, Ton had to tend to her foot several times, as she was not able to do it herself. Her foot dragged along, hanging loose. When they finally managed to crawl about three hundred feet, the Americans opened fire over their heads at the Germans, forcing the enemy to cease shooting and retreat. When the shooting had finally subsided, Ton and Nelly remained in the same spot. After forty-five minutes, a soldier from the American Red Cross came to their aid and attended to Nelly's ankle right away. They brought her to the bridge at Veghel, where immediately more soldiers assisted in taking care of Nelly. She was placed on a stretcher and brought to an emergency hospital near the bridge, where American doctors attended her.

From there, she was transferred to the Veghel hospital, where she regained consciousness only the next afternoon. Ton went home to change clothes and freshen up, and continued with restored faith. The last twenty-four hours had been crucial in penetrating the German blockade of the corridor, and opening the way north. Ton was sent to help evacuate wounded soldiers from the road between Veghel and Uden. The fighting was very fierce; the Germans had regrouped with Panzer divisions, and the war was raging on all sides. Ton attended to a wounded American soldier and found refuge in the house of the Asch family, who were taking refuge in their cellar.

The English had mounted an anti-tank bazooka at the entrance to the house, and were firing at the German tanks only several hundred meters away. The yard was littered with dead chickens as mortars and grenades landed everywhere; the few surviving cows were writhing in pain as they had not been milked for several days. Half of the roof belonging to the Asch's house had been demolished; broken windowpanes, glass, and torn curtains were everywhere. One family member came up to assess the damage as the suffocating heat and lack of ventilation made it quite unbearable in the cellar below. Everyone was on edge, the constant shelling and tremors creating a state of panic and nervousness.

After discussing the options, Ton recommended that the family evacuate as soon as there was a lull in the fighting. He had to try and reach Veghel with his two wounded soldiers. After the shooting had subsided somewhat, the Asch family came upstairs, and fled through the fields with their young children to get well behind the Allied lines. As Ton drove away in a jeep, the shooting recommenced, and was barely a few hundred feet away when a tank shell landed directly on the Asch house, which immediately crumbled. Ton felt a tremendous sense of relief that the family had left just in time.

Ton reached Veghel, but was unable to access the hospital as the English and Americans were attacking a German platoon. He headed for the St. Lambertus Church, and found refuge in the Halls of the Sisters Convent. There were several medics already there, attending other wounded soldiers, who were also waiting to be admitted to the hospital.

Ton observed that the church, to which all his family members belonged, had been badly hit. Apparently the chapel had suffered a direct hit, and the roof around it was full of holes. A grenade had exploded right near the confession booth. Ton met Sister Gijsbertini, who was preparing soup for the people in the numerous cellars underneath the church. She told me that the night before, a grenade was tossed at the cellars underneath the chapel, instantly killing Mietje, the messenger, along with the church's janitor. One of the sisters was seriously wounded and died a few hours later. Another sister, who was preparing food, tried to make it to the cellars when she was hit by a grenade and died. In total, four sisters and two workers lost their lives in yesterday's attack.

During the days that followed, the Allied Forces finally put an end to the Nazi occupation in the Veghel area, but paid an unbelievable price in casualties. Over 17,000 men were either lost, wounded, or had died in "Operation Market Garden." In the Veghel area alone, there were 373 dead American soldiers, 1,436 wounded, and 547 missing in action. The civilian toll in Veghel was not yet known.

Bertie and Susanne were trying to put the pieces of their lives, and their hotel, back together. They were desperate to create a stable and safe environment for their children. Even though it had taken a beating, the hotel was overflowing with people who needed its shelter and the warm attention of the Fox family.

The citizens of Veghel were relieved that at last the enemy had been defeated; they could now focus their attention on rebuilding their lives, and celebrating the defeat of the Germans. The American soldiers looked forward to the coming furlough, and the opportunity to meet the people of the town, for whom they had risked their lives. Bertie and Susanne prepared their bar and kitchen for what they knew was sure to be a grand celebration, but were stopped short when the Americans were ordered to move again, this time north to Nijmegen, where the British had established a frontline.

In the still of the town's thwarted plans, Bertie and Susanne walked around their hotel, surveying the damage to their home and business. Significant repairs would be necessary to restore the hotel back to its former glory; the roof had been destroyed at the rear of the building, and almost the entire second floor had been hit. The billiard table, which was once so heavy that it took at least six men to lift it, had been blown into the air, landing about a foot away from its original moorings. They knew they were lucky to be alive, however, and thanked their lucky stars that no one in their family had been harmed.

Afterwards, they took a look outside at the mayhem. The streets were littered with debris; the windows belonging to familiar buildings had been shattered, and the larger buildings suffered even worse devastation. Round the corner, on the Nieuwstraat, they could see the remains of the church and the complete destruction of the Franciscan Sisters' home. Houses had disintegrated into piles of plaster and stone, and the Ambacht School was left in rubble.

The Americans came to the bombed-out hotel, where most of the citizens of Veghel were gathered, to deliver their sad goodbyes to the people. One of the American officers stood up among the crowd of revellers, cleared his throat, and wished the townspeople well. He thanked them for their help and concern, and declared that even though they had only spent a few short months in Veghel, he and his fellow soldiers had become very attached to the townspeople. Everyone cried as the officer finished his gracious speech, then they bid them farewell with embraces and kisses.

In October, Bertie and Susanne began to plan the rebuilding of their hotel. The rest of the townspeople were occupied in the same venture, working together to restore the collapsed houses on every street. When the British soldiers moved in, the streets took on an entirely different character as soldiers on bicycles, wearing worn leather jackets, posted "KEEP AWAY FROM THE VERGE!" signs throughout the town. They brought their artillery and all the broken tanks they could drag with them into Veghel, which was fast becoming the assemblage line for broken machinery.

Coenen Schoenmakers became the main repair garage where hundreds of young men worked to repair the Sherman tanks. The entire town of Veghel began in earnest to set about repairing and restoring their homes and their lives. Soldiers made plans for their lives after the war. Even the resistance fighters began to integrate back into civilian life. Ton Kuyper, who was put in charge of ordinance between Veghel and Eindhoven, spent a couple of months in hospital, recuperating from a motorcycle accident that took place during a blackout. After fully recuperating, he returned to Veghel to reestablish his bicycle business. Gijs Bossert moved to the west of Holland, and eventually made his fortune in banking.

A very sad report reached the Golden Lion, that Colonel Johnson had been killed on October 8, near Heteren, where he was wounded by shrapnel from a grenade. He died en route to the hospital, with his final words, "Take care of my boys."

Upon hearing the tragic news, everyone in the hotel observed a minute of silence in memory of their great friend and ally. The American troops and the residents of Veghel had paid dearly in their fight for liberty.

REVIVAL OF THE
LIVING DEAD

Chapter 22
A New Life

TO CAROLINE, the small, private room that the JCC had installed her in was the embodiment of luxury. Although the space was confined, able only to accommodate her bed and a small table with two chairs, it had a large, bright window, which allowed in a great deal of sunshine. She could not remember a time when she had her own space, however small, and most importantly, freedom.

She was grateful to the JCC for the apartment and for their help and concern, as everywhere around her Dutch compatriots were trying to put their lives back together again after the devastation of the war. She felt she had been given a fresh start, a new opportunity to rebuild her life.

The past winter had been tough on everyone, and over twenty thousand people in the city had succumbed to its hardships, dying of hunger. Caroline had come very close to becoming such a statistic herself, but she now belonged to the group of survivors. She walked through the war-torn streets, feeling a sense of relief tinged with sorrow and uneasiness. There were some things that you could not recover from. She was on her way to a job interview that the JCC had arranged for her, for a position as a guard in a women's prison, where Dutch NSB collaborators were serving time for their war crimes. Taking a job as a prison guard was somewhat ironic in light of her recent experiences. The prison governor who conducted the interview asked her if she had given this irony any thought.

"I would be lying if I told you that I didn't hate these people," Caroline answered, "but I assure you, I will not let my feelings adversely affect my duties. I need this job desperately, and I will do my best to follow your instructions to the letter."

The commander thought for a moment before informing Caroline that she was to report for her first day at the prison at 8:00 A.M., the following morning.

On her way back from the interview, Caroline made a small detour on the tramway to the center of The Hague. At the Binnenhof station, she looked around for a small, quiet café, and found a pretty one on a nearby corner. She wanted to celebrate her new job by eating a sumptuous, hot breakfast. As she sipped her coffee, she observed the people on the street; mothers fussing over their small children, and businessmen rushing from meeting to meeting. In the distance, a man greeted a woman and kissed her, before they held hands and walked away together. She could not help but think of Soli now, whose image appeared in front of her, as clear as day; she could picture his bright, warm eyes, and his soothing, gentle voice. It had been months since she had allowed herself to remember, but she could no longer block her thoughts and memories of him.

"Is everything all right, miss?" asked the waitress. The girl had come forward when she noticed Caroline sobbing silently into her coffee.

"Yes," said Caroline. "I am fine." She picked herself up and headed for the restroom, where she could cry in private. When she reemerged, she wiped the tears from her eyes and adjusted her lipstick in the mirror. The waitress gave her a quick smile, and offered her another cup of coffee, but Caroline declined.

Next, Caroline wanted to buy a bicycle, with which she could travel to and from work every day, and found one with a delicate little baby's basket attached to the seat. This was the bicycle she wanted to buy. It would be ideal for her and Levie. She imagined herself cycling with him to the park and the beach, laughing together as the wind blew in their hair.

On her first day at work, Caroline was assigned a locker, and was given two fresh uniforms. She was also issued a baton, which was to be used for protection. It came with a silver whistle to be worn on a chain around her neck. When she was dressed in the uniform, Caroline took on the sturdy appearance of the tough prison guard. Tall, stern, and strong, she walked in to meet her new partner, Lidi van Graaf, and face the inmates at the institution for the first time. The twenty-eight inmates of this section were standing to attention, as the governor addressed them:

"I want you all to listen, and listen good. This is Officer Caroline Kanes, and together with Lidi, she will be in charge of you all here. I strongly recommend that you cooperate, as Caroline has survived Dr. Mengele's hell in Auschwitz, and certainly won't take any nonsense from any of you. She has plenty of scores to settle, so I am warning you all!"

One of the prisoners, a tall woman with an authoritative air, called Claudia, sneered, "Are you so hard up for guards that you need Jews to work here now?"

The governor walked over to her, and before anyone realized what had happened, she used her baton to whack her knees, producing a cracking sound and a tremendous wail from the prisoner, who fell to the floor crying and yelling, "You broke my knee, you broke my knee!"

"Next time, you won't be so lucky – I will break your head," the commander replied. "All right, ladies, I hope you have learned your lesson!"

Later, when Caroline and Lidi met with the governor, she asked them how their day had gone. Lidi answered that after that initial incident, the prisoners were on their best behavior and that Claudia had been treated in the infirmary for a minor sprained knee. Caroline had chosen to keep silent, listen, and observe; she did not want her hatred for the prisoners to jeopardize her job. She had only one aim, and that was to get her baby back. She built a good working relationship with Lidi, who was single and invited her several times to join her for drinks in a nice bar near the prison.

Lidi was a good-looking blonde with blue eyes; she was tall and slim, and was constantly attracting the attention of the men around her. Lidi's boyfriend, who had been active in the Underground, had been informed on by the NSB and had been shot by the Nazis, so Lidi had a score to settle as well. Soon Caroline became acclimated to her new life. She worked hard every day at the prison and actively worked to get her son back.

One night, as she was about to sit down to eat dinner, there was a knock at her door. She almost didn't recognize the thin man in the beret who faced her. Suddenly, she realized that the decrepit-looking man was her brother, Ies, who was worse for wear, but still in one piece. She stared at his gaunt face and his silent eyes, and embraced him tightly. Ies was her only link to the past now, which made her more acutely aware of all her other losses. Ies and Caroline ate dinner together, and Caroline told him about her experiences since they had last seen each other. When she had finished, she said, "Papa, Aaron, Wolf, Brametje, Alida, Betsy, Elizabeth, and Soli are all gone, I don't know why I am still alive. Ies, what are we going to do?"

Ies had already grappled with this very question, and was tormented by the gruesome reality that he had been spared, while the others had died. It was a question that would continue to haunt the two remaining siblings for the rest of their lives.

Over coffee, she asked her brother, "Well, Ies, where have you been?" and he replied, "It is more of a case of where I have *not* been!"

Ies proceeded to tell her about his wartime experience: he had joined a resistance unit in France, where he relayed information about troop locations, sabotaged supply lines and bridges, ambushed the enemy, and harried the occupying forces as they retreated eastwards in the face of the Allied invasion. In the beginning, the French locals thought Ies was a bandit, who was scrounging for food, but they finally began to understand what he had actually been doing over the last year. Then, the local population took great pains to supply food and clothing to Ies and his men.

Finally, Ies was shot during a confrontation with German troops, and was transferred to a hospital, where they extracted the bullet from his leg and allowed him to recuperate. He explained to the doctors and nurses that his first priority was to find his family.

"Clientje," he said eagerly, "I know that we have lost so much, but we have to focus our efforts now on finding Levie."

Now that Ies had returned, and offered his support and help in finding Levie, Caroline felt a surge of renewed hope that she would be reunited with her son. The two agreed to eat dinner together every night at her apartment. That night, Caroline's head was buzzing with all the life changes she had to adjust to recently, and she had mixed feelings about her current situation. On the one hand, she felt safe and secure again now that Ies had returned, and she clung onto the hope that she would see her son again. She knew that it would just be a matter of time before Levie would be found, and eventually returned to her.

Chapter 23
On the Run

Veghel, 1946

NOW THAT THE WAR was over, and Susanne and Bertie were busy rebuilding their lives after the war, Susanne began to think about the subject of "war orphans." Although she kept herself busy in the hotel, and with the children, talk of returning these children now circulated in a disturbing way. She could not bear the thought of losing Jantje, who was like a son to her. Tilly warned Susanne and Bertie about the JCC, and Bram de Jong's efforts to reunite, whenever possible, Jewish children with their parents. The aim was for "war orphans" to be returned to their biological parents, but that they would maintain a relationship with their foster/adoptive parents, who had raised them through difficult times. Tilly told Susanne about a bill that the Resistance wanted to pass, whereby foster/adoptive parents of Jewish children would be recognized as the true parents, especially if their biological parents who had survived the war were too traumatized by their experiences to be able to care for their children. The members of the Resistance were active in establishing a central bureau in Amsterdam, in which the needs of such children would be addressed.

Like Susanne and Bertie, there were so many foster parents who had risked their lives to provide shelter for these children, and they had developed very strong feelings of responsibility and love for them. This

177

being the case, the new regulations had to display a sensitivity towards foster parents, who, they hoped, would not refuse to return their children to their biological parents.

Tilly advised Susanne that she should hold onto Jantje, and not even return him to his biological parents, until she received guidelines from the central bureau. Susanne and Bertie were terrified. They had known all along that the day would come when they would have to consider giving Jantje up, but they had banished this prospect from their minds, believing that if they denied that the problem existed, then it did not actually exist. During the war, they had discovered that Jantje's biological parents were sent East, from where few returned, so they deluded themselves into thinking that Jantje would remain with them permanently. Tilly tried to reassure Bertie and Susanne by informing them of the law that stated that parents who did not report their missing children within one month of the war did not have the right to reclaim them. Tilly assured them that the Church was very supportive of the Resistance, and also of the families who had hidden the children. Many church leaders nurtured the hope that since these children had been raised in the Catholic faith, they should remain Catholics. Susanne and Bertie tried not to allow themselves to give into fear, but anticipated the worst. In the meantime, they focused their efforts on planning Jan's baptism, which was to take place in the rebuilt St. Lambertus Church, and shopped for his christening suit with Tilly. The day the baptism took place was sunny and warm, and after the ceremony, the Foxes hosted a wonderful party at the Golden Lion, where family and friends lavished their attention on Jantje, showering him with gifts and toys.

Susanne had not given Jan's biological parents a second thought until she heard her son's name being mentioned on a radio announcement. On that day, she was working away in the kitchen when she heard the words, "Levie Kanes" and "Office of Lost War Children" being uttered in the same sentence. She heard talk of meetings and regulations and custody, but Susanne didn't stay long enough in the kitchen to listen to the end of the announcement. Within half an hour, she and Jantje were on their way to another town, where they could hide, leaving behind her husband and daughter. Susanne continued to flee from one town to another in order to ensure that Jan remained with her for good.

After running from town to town with Jantje, Susanne finally found a secluded hiding place in a monastery, where she was completely sheltered from the outside world and inaccessible to all, save the nuns on site. There, months passed before the Mother Superior advised Susanne strongly that she must return to Veghel and hire a lawyer to help her, as word had it that Susanne was summoned to appear in court to face Caroline Kanes. The nun sadly informed Susanne that the Church could not aid and abet her unlawful actions, in keeping the boy from his biological mother; one way or another, Susanne would have to return home and resolve the situation.

Meanwhile, Caroline had phoned Bram de Jong several times to inquire about Levie, but the answer remained the same: she had to be patient. They were working on the case and making steady progress; they would meet with her in about fifteen days.

Several days later, Caroline was sitting with Ies when the phone rang. It was Bram from the JCC with great news: "We have located your son Levie, he is fine, and we are in touch with the foster family. We will keep you informed within the next few days when you can go and see him. Hopefully, you will get him back soon."

As she heard the good news, Caroline felt a mixture of relief and delight surge right through her. She shared the news with Ies, and they agreed to travel to Brabant together as soon as the JCC gave them the green light.

Meanwhile, Susanne spent the next few weeks in her home village of Erp, with her sister Jeannette. Here Jantje had a great time as he had both his Aunt Jeannette and his grandfather to spoil him. Susanne, on the other hand, was a nervous wreck, and was practically glued to the radio, following the latest developments regarding war orphans. She had heard that several foster children had been returned to their birth parents through the intervention of the courts, and she felt very insecure about her situation. She spoke to Bertie who informed her that a local police officer, accompanied by a court clerk, came to visit them at the hotel. They wanted to make sure that Levie Kanes was not their foster child, since Levie's biological mother, who had returned from the camps, was attempting to regain parental custody of him.

"What did you tell them?" Susanne asked.

"I told them that you had gone away for a short vacation, and as soon as you return, you will call them."

Susanne panicked at the news, and packed her suitcase with some clothes for her and Jantje, and told her sister that she was returning to Veghel. Of course, she never intended to go home to Veghel, but instead travelled to Druten where her sister Lena lived. She filled Lena in on the situation, and made her swear not to tell any of the family where she was located.

Several days passed until Lena told Susanne that the police had been to their father's home looking for her, and had questioned neighbors regarding her whereabouts.

"They may find me here, so I will move on, and so as not to implicate you, I won't tell you where I am going. Thanks for all your help."

Susanne hugged her sister and left with Jantje. She proceeded to the central bus station, where she phoned her sister Tilly, who was now at the Franciscan monastery in Reuzel. After briefly explaining the situation, she was told to phone back in fifteen minutes so that Tilly could check with the Mother Superior if Susanne and Jantje could hide at the monastery. Tilly called back, and to Susanne's relief, received permission for her to come. She took her baby and her bags, and boarded a bus to Reuzel.

Susanne finally found relief at the monastery, where she was completely sheltered from the outside world, and as the weeks passed, she started to feel at ease. As for Jantje, he was very happy with all the attention the Sisters were lavishing on him. He was a real little rascal. He loved to climb up to the towers of the monastery, and swing on the ropes that descended from the huge bells above. Jantje squealed with delight as the sisters rushed up the towers to stop the bells from chiming. But Jantje could do no wrong; he was the darling of all the sisters, who loved having a sweet little boy around the place.

After six weeks, Tilly told Susanne that the Mother Superior wanted to see them. She entered her office with a heavy heart. Mother Superior sadly told Susanne that the Church could not act as an accomplice to her plans to keep the boy unlawfully separated from his mother, and that she would have to return home. Susanne had no choice but to return to Veghel.

Bertie was happy and relieved to see Susanne and Jantje, and he embraced them both. He showed his wife the court summons that ordered her to appear for a hearing at the district court of Amsterdam, on December 20, 1946, where she would have to face Caroline's claim that the child they had been raising as their own since April 1943 was in fact her son, Levie.

"Oh, Bert, what will we do?" Susanne sobbed.

Bertie attempted to comfort his wife. "We will hire the best lawyer," he whispered.

Chapter 24
The Fight for Levie Kanes

CAROLINE WAS DISTRAUGHT to hear from Bram that her son's adopted mother had run away with him, but was relieved to hear that the authorities were trying to locate them. Bram urged her to be patient; he was convinced that it was just a matter of time until she would be reunited with her child for good.

"She can't hide forever, and she will be arrested if she does not present herself to the authorities soon. Believe me, the authorities are doing everything they can to locate her."

Ies consoled and comforted his sister. "Look, Clientje, this woman just panicked. Imagine yourself in her shoes – what would you do if you had raised a child as your own for two years, only to have to give him back? At least this shows us that Levie is in good hands. This woman must love him very much to leave her husband and daughter and go into hiding!"

The next weeks were nerve-wracking; Caroline was desperate to see her child and started having graphic nightmares about her experiences at Auschwitz. Ies took her to a specialist who prescribed her some sedatives. Within a couple of days, they were called in for an urgent meeting with Bram.

"Good news!" Bram reported when Caroline and Ies arrived. "We have a court hearing for December 20, at the district court of Amsterdam, where you will have to prove that the child now called Johannes Maria Fox is really your son Levie Kanes."

As Bram served them coffee, he took out Caroline's file to discuss the upcoming hearing. "Here we have a copy of the police constable's report detailing the events of the night of April 12, 1943, when a nurse had handed him a child, whose mother was being transported to Westerbork. He delivered the baby to a courier called Joop Wortman, and he recorded that the baby was still wearing an identity bracelet from the hospital in The Hague, which read 'Levie Kanes, 25-1-43.' The infant was then delivered to a courier in The Hague called Zus Pare, who, together with Father Theo Verhoeven, delivered the child to the Fox family in Veghel, the proprietors of the Golden Lion Hotel."

Bram continued: "What interests me is that in her report, Zus Pare wrote that the infant was circumcised, and had a red welt on his right hip, signifying that he had undergone an operation! What can you tell me about this?" Bram inquired.

Caroline felt her heart hammering away in her chest. "Levie needed to have kidney stones removed from his bladder, which is why they kept me in the hospital for a while longer. After Levie had recuperated from his operation, we were sent to Westerbork. The hospital must have some record of Levie's operation!"

"Wonderful!" Bram exclaimed. "I will have the hospital records checked, and have already asked the court to subpoena Zus Pare, Theo Verhoeven, Joop Wortman, and the constable, so my dear friends, I think we will be able to prove in court that the infant in question is your son, Levie."

"Bram, what do you want us to do now?" Ies asked.

"Just meet me in court. I will bring all the documents and proof, and the director of our legal department will be there to present your case to the judges. Also, please bring a letter of recommendation from your place of work and your pledge, Ies, to help support your sister in rearing Levie. That way, we will be able to shield ourselves from the claim that Caroline cannot single-handedly raise Levie."

Caroline and Ies left the meeting in high spirits, and for the first time in what seemed like forever, Caroline felt optimistic.

"Ies, let's stop on the way home, and celebrate the good news with a drink," she suggested.

He replied, "You know that I do not need convincing!"

As they relaxed over a few drinks, they started to discuss their family. Ies had been searching for any family members that might have survived the Holocaust, and informed Caroline of what he had discovered.

"For starters, I have traced a couple of nephews. As you know, Wolf and Betsy's son, Haim, is living with his foster parents in Rotterdam. He apparently is doing very well. Your sister-in-law, Anna Kanes, had left her baby, Kalman, with a family in Hilversum. Both your nephews are living with financially stable people, but they are not being raised to be Jewish. I think that our next aim, after we get Levie back, is to work on getting them back, too."

Caroline and Ies met Bram and their legal counsel at the courts on December 20, and were informed that the Fox family had arrived with their lawyer and were inside the chambers. They proceeded at once to the assigned chamber, and as they entered, Caroline saw two men and a woman sitting inside, and suspected that this was the Fox couple with their lawyer. She was proven correct as they rose when the judge entered the chambers, and the court clerk read out the claim of Caroline Kanes Nathan versus Bertie and Susanne Fox of the Golden Lion Hotel, Veghel.

Susanne was sworn in as she took the stand, and was asked by her attorney to tell the court her version of the events. Susanne was extremely nervous. She could feel her heart pounding away, but she knew that she had to try to win the judge's sympathy, if she were to keep her little son. She told the court how she had received a very sick two-month-old baby in April 1943, whom she had nursed back to health. She told how Bertie had threatened the local doctor with a gun if he refused to treat their circumcised baby. She continued to explain how the child had adapted easily to his new environment, and that he was now a healthy, happy child. He loved Bertie and her, and was crazy about Lia, his sister.

"This leaves no doubt, your honor," Susanne testified, "that taking him away from us will cause tremendous psychological damage to the child, which could make him very ill, as a result. Our son has been baptized and is a member of the Catholic religion, so it would be morally reprehensible to take him away from his faith. And finally, I beseech you to have pity on my family; taking our son away from us would be like removing one of my limbs. I don't think I could survive the ordeal."

The judge asked Susanne if she was aware of her baby's true identity.

"How can we be sure? I was told that his parents had perished in the camps," she replied.

The judge continued, "Does your baby have a scar on his right hip?"

"Yes, your honor," Susanne quietly replied.

The judge thanked her, and asked her to stand down.

The attorney representing the Foxes asked permission to present a psychiatrist's report that confirmed the child's healthy state of mind, and warned that removing the child from his environment at this stage would be detrimental to the child's mental state. He recommended that, for the good of the child, he remain with the Fox family.

The court then called on Caroline's lawyer, who asked Ies to testify on behalf of Caroline, as she was in no fit state to tell her tale. Once sworn in, Ies proceeded to tell the court how his sister had given birth on January 25, 1943 at the Haagse General Hospital, and remained there for a few months, because Levie had to have his kidney stones removed. Consequently, they were discharged from the hospital on April 12, 1943, and were transported to Westerbork Transit Camp. On the way, the train stopped in Utrecht, where Dutch nurses were permitted to board to attend to some of the ill passengers.

"My sister watched as one of the nurses smuggled her baby to safety, convinced that this was his only chance for survival. She watched as the nurse descended from the train, carrying the bamboo basket with some bandages and the baby inside, and watched her pass the basket to a Dutch policeman, just as the train continued on its journey."

He told of her reunion with her husband in Westerbork, and how they were separated in Auschwitz. Once there, she endured horrifying experiences in Block 10, where she was subjected to cruel and torturous experiments that no human being should ever have to bear. Her will to survive was based on her dreams of getting her baby back.

"She had lost her whole family, her husband, brothers and sisters, and the thought of her baby kept her going, against all odds. Your honor, didn't this woman suffer enough? Should she be punished additionally by having her child kept away from her, a child who is one of the few survivors of the Kanes family, who, prior to the Holocaust, numbered more than five hundred? We are very grateful to the Fox family for the love and kindness that they showed Levie, but he now belongs with his biological mother."

Evidence was then presented, confirming that Caroline was financially

stable, with a secure job, and that her brother Ies also accepted the responsibility of taking care of his nephew's needs. They also presented a written
commitment from The Hague Jewish community, that vouched to provide
Caroline Kanes with financial aid, as long as she needed it, and a letter of
recommendation from the governor of the women's prison in Scheveningen,
which confirmed that Caroline was a reliable and responsible guard.

The judge then asked the attorneys to approach the bench, where he
told them that there was no doubt that the child in question is Levie Kanes,
but that the defense is hinging its case on the welfare of the child, and the
law that was passed which stated that parents who fail to report their missing child are probably incapable of competently assuming their parental
duties, and have no right to reclaim their biological children until they are
deemed fit to do so by the courts. Receiving confirmation from the Fox's
attorney, the judge informed them that in this case, testimony from the
other witnesses is unnecessary, since the baby's identity had already been
proven. He announced that he would take an hour's recess to consider the
details of the case.

Caroline felt as if a rope was being tightened around her neck; the
tension was killing her. Ies, who sensed her nervousness, tried to put her
at ease. He assured her that the verdict would be in their favor. After what
seemed like an eternity to Caroline, the judge returned and read out his
verdict.

"Since it has been established that the identity of the child in question
is Levie Kanes, son of Solomon Kanes, deceased, and Caroline Kanes nee
Nathan, here present with counsel, the court's responsibility is to oversee
the welfare of the child. There is no doubt that the child has had the good
fortune to have been raised by such a loving and caring family as the
Foxes, and that the return to his biological mother will be quite traumatic
for the child. Nevertheless the court feels that the child belongs with his
mother who has proved herself to be a very courageous and responsible
person, who will be able to adequately look after her child. To assure the
child's welfare, the court places the child under the supervision of the child
welfare division, and will have regular visits from the social worker who
will furnish the court with monthly reports of the child's progress over a
period of twenty-four months. I do want to express the court's gratitude
to the Fox family for their courage and devotion to the child, and strongly
recommend that Mrs. Kanes should keep in touch with them, so that they

may visit Levie. The social worker will accompany Mrs. Kanes next Monday morning 10:00 A.M. to pick up the child in Veghel."

Caroline felt a surge of relief and joy that she had not felt in many years. She fell into her brother's arms, sobbing from happiness and joy, and thanked Bram and the legal team for their help in recovering her child.

On the other side of the courtroom, Susanne sank into her seat. She felt as if the world was collapsing around her. She felt faint, and although Bertie was doing his best to try and comfort her, he too felt shattered inside.

FULL CIRCLE

Chapter 25
As Told By Levie

THIS IS WHERE my story begins, since it is only at this point that I can truly remember the drastic changes that were to affect my life forever. I recall playing in the yard with my sister, Lia, and Tarzan, our dog, when Mama and Papa returned home. They had been gone for a few days, and Aunt Tilly was looking after us. I saw Mama descending from the taxi, wearing a dark suit and hat, looking very serious. As she spotted me, she ran over and swooped me up in her arms, and began to tremble and cry as she squeezed me hard. I sensed something was wrong, as I was getting all wet from Mama's tears. The next few days were very eerie and somber – everyone looked so upset. Even my best friend, Jack the cook, was unusually serious and sad. I asked him what was wrong, what had I done that everyone seemed so serious? Jack explained to me that my real mother had returned from the camps, and was going to take me back to The Hague with her on Monday morning. At first, I did not understand what he meant, as I knew my Mama and Papa were Susanne and Bertie, but eventually I grasped that a Jewish woman, who claimed to be my mother, was awarded custody of me, and I would have to go with her.

I hoped that Monday would never come, but to no avail. That morning, Tilly packed a little suitcase containing my clothes, and another bag with some of my favorite toys, and dressed me in a blue and white navy suit that I would wear to church. I could see a car stop in front of the hotel, and Father Verhoeven got out, accompanied by a tall woman and a man. They were met by Bertie, and realizing that they were here to take me away, I ran to the yard, and grabbed Tarzan's kennel, in the hope that they would forget about me. That morning, Mama had told me what would happen and begged me to be a good boy, and that she would visit me very often. I felt as if the world was coming to an end. There I was, a little boy holding on with all his might to his dog's kennel in order to prevent this woman from taking me away with her. As they pried me loose, I started to kick the woman and screamed, "You are not my Mama, I am not Jewish, I don't want to go with you," but there was no point. I was lifted by the man and carried into the car, and was screaming and crying as we left the Golden Lion. I saw Mama, Papa, and Lia crying in front of the hotel, watching as we drove away.

Chapter 26
A New Identity

IT WAS NOT EASY adjusting to my new life. It would take me a long time before I could feel at ease around my new mother, and I was rebellious, both at home and in school. My biological mother shared a house on the Geleenstraat, with David Kallus, a widower whose wife, Johanna, and their two daughters, Hermina and Flora, only four- and five-years old, had been killed in Auschwitz on September 21, 1942. David had survived hard labor in Auschwitz, and ended up cleaning up the devastation of the Warsaw Ghetto. He was an austere and harsh man, who hardly spoke at all. Each day, he left early for the kosher butcher shop, where he was the *mashgiach* [supervisor of kosher standards]. Times had been very hard since the end of the war, since everything was scarce, but we were lucky that my mother's uncle from Hartford, Connecticut, would send us large wooden crates filled with nylon stockings, clothes, all kinds of canned food, and, of course, large blue jars of Maxwell House Coffee. These items were like precious jewels, and my mother sold them in no time on the black market, where they fetched handsome prices.

I was sent to a Jewish school on the Waagenstraat, and had a very difficult time learning Hebrew and Jewish prayers. I was obsessed with returning to Veghel. The only person who helped me overcome my problems was my Uncle Ies. He was everything a father should be – kind, understanding, patient and above all, very loving. He dedicated much of his free time to taking me to all kinds of fairs and parks. He spoiled me, bought me many toys, and sent me to summer camp during July and August. He helped me convince my mother to let Lia come and stay with us for a week during school vacation, and he would take us everywhere. I was so excited when Bertie showed up with Lia, and fell in his arms, whispering, "How is Mama?" I could see the tears welling up in his eyes as he told me that she was fine, and asked me to have a good time with Lia.

We had an unforgettable week, thanks to Lia, and especially Uncle Ies, who outdid himself in catering to our every need. After this time with my sister, my mother saw to it that I did not have any more contact with my family in Veghel. She did not want to be reminded of the hardships she had endured to get me back, and did not want them to have any further contact with me. I was then made aware that I had two cousins my own age, Charles Land, born Kalman Bruinvelds Kanes, and Harry Pulleman, born Haim Nathan. They were both living with their foster parents. After the war had ended, my mother had applied to the courts for custody of her two nephews, but eventually gave up as she already had her hands full with one rebellious child, and satisfied herself with visiting rights.

It was a cold night in October 1947 when Ies informed us that he was leaving for France with four of his Jewish friends from Rotterdam. The plan was to travel from France to Palestine, where they would help defend the country against the Jews' Arab neighbors. Dutch law did not permit its citizens to join foreign military forces under penalty of forfeiting one's citizenship. As far as the Dutch Immigration Office was concerned, Ies was in France.

It was tense times as we waited for some news or a postcard from Uncle Ies. Finally, at the end of May 1948, we received a postcard from Ies, informing us that he was well and would be returning home in several months.

Uncle Ies returned in September, sunburned and very thin, and told me all about his combat experiences in the Sinai desert, stopping the Egyptian advance with his unit. I adored my uncle, who had always filled me with pride for his heroism.

The next thing I heard was that my mother was going to marry David Kallus in February 1949. The rabbinate had objected to the two of them living under the same roof, so he moved out, only to return as my mother's new husband. I was told that I could not attend the ceremony, as this was not allowed, but that I could come to the party afterwards at the synagogue hall.

My mother miraculously became pregnant, even after all the experiments she had endured in Auschwitz, and on July 11, 1950, my sister Henriette Kallus was born.

A year later came the news that was to become the second trauma in my life: I was informed that David Kallus had decided to emigrate to Canada, and that we would be sailing from Rotterdam on the *Nieuw Amsterdam* on February 20, 1952.

The months leading to our departure for Canada were hectic, but at least my uncle Ies took me to Veghel to bid farewell to my family. This was an unforgettable visit for me. It was the last time I was to see all the family together.

Finally the dreaded date arrived. Uncle Ies accompanied us to the ship, which weighed 36,000 tons, one of the biggest ships in the world at the time, with five floors and four elevators. I stood at the bough, where I waved goodbye to my uncle, who was like a father to me, and as the boat departed, his figure became increasingly distant. I was never to see him again.

Caroline Kanes remarries David Kallus in The Hague, February 1949

Caroline Kanes and Levie, The Hague, 1947

Ies in his Israeli army uniform, Israel, 1948

Zus Pare and Levie Kanes at the author's wedding, Israel, June 1963

Susanne Fox, shortly before her death in Veghel, 2000

Chapter 27

The Next Soly Kanes Tells His Story

Israel, Border with Lebanon, 1985

"WE ARE LEAVING in another seven minutes. There is a high security alert in the area, so make sure that everything is in order – guns, grenades, etc. – and board the transport vehicle," sounded the booming voice of the sergeant. I quickly closed my helmet, and grabbed my arms and bullet-proof vest. The transport took off and I was ready. My eyes scanned the surroundings, and the cold wind made my eyes tear. As I prepared to go to the battlefront, I felt grateful that I had the fortune to be a fighter, and had the right to live or die with honor.

By 15:30 hours, we had reached Jub Jenin near the Caroun Lake. The transport veered strongly to the right, and after a few minutes, passed a security gate and stopped next to our tents. Not even a minute had passed, when a shout was heard:

"Corporal Solomon Kanes!"

"That's me," I answered fast. Suddenly, the sergeant major, a large towering figure, appeared in front of me. He looked like he was in need of a rest. His face told the tale.

"Are you a combat medic?" he inquired.

"Yes sir," I replied.

"Listen, I will tell you straight. I understand that you are new here, but we have a problem you can help us with at this moment."

"Yes, sir?"

"We have a problematic *mutsav* [outpost] at a volatile front. Yesterday the medic was killed, so we no longer have a combat medic, and you can imagine what will happen if we are ambushed tonight. This is a seasoned veteran combat unit, and I am sure you will have no problem fighting alongside them."

"No problem, sir, with pleasure," I replied.

"Get something hot to drink, get on the halftrack, and join the unit. You should make sure to get there before dark. You can eat later when you get there so as not to lose time now," the sergeant major ordered.

"Yes sir," I replied, with a slight smile spreading across my face. I was excited at the prospect of joining a top unit.

After a shaky ride, the back gate of the halftrack opened at the *mutsav* on the mountain. I arrived at the Gamal el Luz Outlook on the Lebanon-Syria border at 20:00 hours.

"*Baruch habah*," a captain said, offering me a welcome with his out-stretched hand. "I am Eli, the commanding officer of the *mutsav*, and I am glad that you are with us." After a short exchange of words, I understood why this was a problematic *mutsav*. The unit's combat medic had been killed the day before, and he was the third medic to have lost his life at this post in the last month. The mission seemed so important that it was overwhelming, and I felt exhilarated at the thought of the task in front of me.

After receiving orders with the rest of the unit, we started out on our mission, which passed without incident. The excitement of the first day made me very tired and I was looking forward to lying down for a rest. That night, I slept only two and a half hours. At 2:30 A.M., I was given permission to sleep until 5:00 A.M., when I would resume duty. I crept into my sleeping bag fully clothed, and fell asleep.

The smell of fire made me suddenly jump to my feet. Within seconds, I left the tent confused, and I fell into a trench, and felt my clothes on fire. I instinctively started to run inside the *mutsav*.

"Lie down on the sand," a voice called out to me. I listened to the instructions, and rolled over onto the floor. After a short check, I found out that I had not been burned, but was alive as well.

"Medic, medic," I heard someone calling.

I followed the sound of the voice, and saw three of my comrades wounded on the ground. I checked Rafi first, and found shrapnel in his stomach. I bandaged him quickly and in a way so that he would not feel too much pain in the transfer to the hospital. Then I approached Raul and Yossi, and saw that they were only lightly wounded. Clear orders sounded, and we understood that a rocket from one of the heights in the area had been fired upon the *mutsav*.

We went after them. "You have three minutes to get your backpack ready," ordered the officer. After Yossi and Raul received a blood infusion, I ran with my weapons and the stretcher on my back to join the rest of the unit. The descent from the mountain was steep and on the way we were briefed on the situation by night spotters, who told us that our attackers had entered a residential home after the curfew. Within six minutes, we reached the house. Eli, the officer, ordered three soldiers to cover us, and the officer led five men, including myself, into the house. We readied our weapons and stood close to the entrance, next to the house. The officer went in first, followed by me. I stood to the right. I wondered whether I would come out of this alive.

"*Kadima*," ordered the officer. "Forward."

Carefully, he went in. I waited ten seconds, then with a strong blow, I crashed through the door and rushed in with my M-16. Immediately I saw a man, about thirty years of age, aiming his gun at me. I opened fire and shot him with several dozen bullets. Then I aimed at the bed where a frightened eighteen-year-old girl sat, but I realized that she was only a poor victim of circumstance.

In a soft voice, I asked her in Arabic, "*Kulo Kwajish?*" – "Is everything all right?" She replied, shivering, "*Kwajesh, shukran*" – "I am fine, thank you."

I went to my comrades, and saw that we had killed three more of the enemy and that none of our men had been wounded. The officer ordered us to return immediately to attend to the wounded, and transport them to a hospital. This was a difficult task as the helicopter had problems reaching the area, and the bulk of the medical responsibility fell on me. There was no doctor anywhere nearby. A halftrack was given permission to take the wounded and after replenishing our stock of equipment and bullets, I went to the foot of the mountain to sit down for a moment and sipped some water from my canteen. The tranquility of the wind pacified me, and through the wind, I saw a *demut*, a kind of phantom. It was me in my earlier *gilgul* [incarnation], laughing with satisfaction at the opportunity afforded me this time. I found myself with a painted face, forming part of a circle where feet met, and at the first sign of the enemy, the spotter would kick the other feet as a sign. We finally returned to the camp and I was grateful for the chance to have a good night's rest.

Exhausted, I lay down, and as I began to fall into a deep sleep, I thought back to my family and my childhood. In my mind, I was eight years old again, and was practicing in my father's boxing gym in Costa Rica. My father, Levie Kanes, had been the boxing manager for Roberto "Mano de Piedra" Duran, the world lightweight champion. I remembered visiting him at the gym, while Duran was preparing to defend his world title in San José, Costa Rica, against Masataka Takayama from Japan. Being the son of Levie Kanes had its advantages, as my father was a famous, powerful figure who appeared almost daily on talk shows, and was loved by the sporting community of Costa Rica for reviving boxing to heights no Central American country had ever reached, not to mention managing one of the main soccer teams in the country.

My mother, on the other hand, was far more reserved than my father, but she was blessed with both intelligence and great beauty. I was thrilled when my friends in school quoted the television announcer who reported that last night, the *Gimnasio National* was packed to the brim, with half of the public there to see Duran fight and the other half to watch Kanes's wife.

I also thought back to my parents' description of how they had met. The first time they laid eyes on each other was on a ship sailing to Israel in April 1961. My mom was travelling from Costa Rica with her grandparents, and my dad, who had come from Montreal by train, was on his way to Israel to check out kibbutz life. My father spotted my mom on the boat, standing with Ilana, another girl he had met on board, watching the Statue of Liberty. He approached the two girls, and asked Ilana, "Hi, who's your good-looking friend?"

"Oh," she answered, "this is Ofelia, but she only speaks Spanish!" Luckily, they both knew some Yiddish. It was love at first sight. After two years in Israel, and once my dad finished his voluntary army service, they married on D-Day, June 6, 1963. My sister Etty was born a year later, they returned to Montreal, where I was born, and in 1967, they relocated to Costa Rica, where my brother Ies was born in 1975.

I remembered when a year later, in 1968, my mother announced that we were moving to Israel, as we had saved enough money to buy a house there and start a business. At first I was very unhappy at the thought of moving, but once in Israel, we adjusted very quickly. I grew up in a *moshav*, a communal settlement, called Kfar Haroeh, where motivation ran high, and children looked forward to joining some special unit of the armed forces. My father had let me know more than once that his greatest hope was to see me become an officer and a leader.

Suddenly I was jolted out of my memories, and heard someone shouting, "Kanes, Kanes, let's move it! There are wounded soldiers that need you." I was up and ready within minutes, and the breeze in the speeding jeep invigorated me.

Mitzpeh Ramon, 1987

It was a great day. My family had travelled the 200 km to Mitzpeh Ramon in the south of Israel to attend the officers' graduation ceremony, and my father was overjoyed that finally he had a son who served as an officer in the Israeli Defense Forces. General Yitzhak Rabin placed my officer's badge on my shoulder pad. I joined my family. My father hugged me and told me that when the national anthem *Hatikva* was being played, and the Israeli flag was blowing in the wind, it was one of the most touching moments of his life. He thought how proud the souls of his father, Soli Kanes, and his uncle, Ies Nathan, would be today to see the first Kanes inducted as an officer in the Israeli Defense Forces, where Jews could finally defend themselves.

I think that this was one of the most special days of my father's life. The memory of the Holocaust was etched in his memory, and his raison d'etre was for his children to serve in the Israeli Defense Forces in mind of the perished Kanes clan. I felt proud that, at last, I had lived up to my father's expectations.

Levie Kanes with his wife, Ofelia, by the Western Wall, Jerusalem, 2003

Soly Kanes in his Israeli army uniform, Israel, 1987

Afterword

I T WAS NEW YEARS DAY, and our family had gathered to greet the new year and millennium. I first turned to my wife Ofelia. Thirty-six years of marriage had made her more beautiful than ever, and I thanked God once again for giving me this wonderful partner who was instrumental in the positive development of our children.

I felt great tonight seeing the Kanes clan and the new generation. My oldest daughter, Etty, is a strong determined woman, quite like her late grandmother Caroline. She holds a senior position in a local exporting firm, while running a household with her husband, Yair. They have two wonderful children, Caroline and Arie Raphael. Then I looked at Soly, with his wife Ayala, and their sons, Meir and Haim Orr. From everything I had ever heard about my father, Soly resembles him most, both in looks and personality. Their similarity to each other sometimes makes me wonder if reincarnation is possible.

I looked at my next son, Ies, who is named after my dear uncle. Standing at a striking six-foot-seven, he not only shares his uncle's name, but his namesake's great heart and patriotism for Israel. Our family returned to Costa Rica just as Ies was to enter the army. Although he could have gone with us, Ies remained in Israel on his own to enter military service.

He was distinguished as the outstanding soldier of the military police, and was given the highest award on Israeli Independence Day by Prime Minister Yitzhak Rabin. Ies's mother, Ofelia, had flown to Israel to attend this ceremony, and was invited to the President's home for the occasion. Ies was there with Jenny, his wife, who he married in August 1999. Like Ofelia, she is beautiful and has an exceptional character. As I looked at them, I secretly hoped that they would provide us with some more Kaneses!

Nearby stood my daughter Elizabeth Regina. Tall and slender, and blessed with her mother's beauty, she is a great girl, studying for a degree in social work in the university. Next to her was her sister Aliza, our foster daughter, who has been with us since she was just six-months old. She is a gift from God, a sweet and wonderful girl who thrives on the love and care we give her, and has become a confident and successful person.

As I finish writing this book, I can only say that my children, who are fine and caring people, give honor to the Kanes name. May they continue to grow as upstanding citizens.

AUTHOR'S NOTE: During publication of this book, Ies and Jenny had two children, Omri Kanes and Sapir Malka Kanes. Aliza married David Michaeli and gave birth to a son, Or Meir Michaeli. Elizabeth Regina married Ofer Hoffman.

In Memoriam

Canes/Kanes family members who perished in the Holocaust:

	DATE OF BIRTH	PLACE OF BIRTH	DATE OF DEATH	PLACE OF DEATH
Canes, Aaron	06-10-1912	Amsterdam	30-09-1942	Auschwitz
Canes, Abraham	06-12-1898	Amsterdam	02-04-1943	Sobibor
Canes, Abraham	11-08-1918	Amsterdam	01-09-1943	Mauthausen
Canes, Abraham	15-11-1925	Amsterdam	30-09-1942	Auschwitz
Canes, Alex	16-03-1926	Amsterdam	25-01-1943	Auschwitz
Canes, Antoon	06-05-1904	Amsterdam	21-01-1945	Blechhammer
Canes, Aron	18-11-1905	Amsterdam	29-02-1944	Auschwitz
Canes, Aron	06-10-1925	Amsterdam	30-09-1942	Auschwitz
Canes, Barend	11-01-1933	Amsterdam	11-06-1943	Sobibor
Canes, Benjamin	21-01-1892	Amsterdam	09-07-1943	Sobibor
Canes, Bertha	22-03-1911	Amsterdam	03-09-1943	Auschwitz
Canes, Betje	11-03-1883	Amsterdam	08-10-1942	Auschwitz
Canes, Betsij	09-08-1903	Amsterdam	28-05-1943	Sobibor
Canes, Branca	09-06-1927	Amsterdam	19-10-1942	Auschwitz
Canes, Celina	09-10-1918	Amsterdam	30-09-1942	Auschwitz
Canes, Clara	21-03-1916	Amsterdam	24-09-1943	Auschwitz

	DATE OF BIRTH	PLACE OF BIRTH	DATE OF DEATH	PLACE OF DEATH
Canes, Clara	30-04-1927	Amsterdam	30-09-1942	Auschwitz
Canes, David	19-04-1872	Amsterdam	05-02-1943	Auschwitz
Canes, David	24-09-1919	Amsterdam	18-07-1941	Mauthausen
Canes, David	24-05-1921	Amsterdam	30-09-1942	Auschwitz
Canes, Elisabeth	26-05-1901	Amsterdam	30-04-1943	Sobibor
Canes, Elisabeth	21-08-1914	Amsterdam	30-09-1942	Auschwitz
Canes, Emanuel	22-11-1870	Amsterdam	14-09-1942	Auschwitz
Canes, Emanuel	31-07-1924	Amsterdam	08-08-1942	Auschwitz
Canes, Esther	24-07-1890	Amsterdam	22-05-1944	Auschwitz
Canes, Esther	06-05-1902	Amsterdam	30-09-1942	Auschwitz
Canes, Eva	20-11-1920	Amsterdam	04-06-1943	Sobibor
Canes, Gerrit	21-05-1927	Amsterdam	31-12-1942	Auschwitz
Canes, Hartog	04-09-1897	Amsterdam	31-05-1944	Auschwitz
Canes, Heintje	25-10-1875	Amsterdam	14-09-1942	Auschwitz
Canes, Heintje	22-04-1899	Amsterdam	04-06-1943	Sobibor
Canes, Heintje	02-03-1905	Amsterdam	28-05-1943	Sobibor
Canes, Heintje	02-02-1917	Amsterdam	12-10-1942	Auschwitz
Canes, Heintje Elisabeth	05-08-1935	Amsterdam	19-11-1942	Auschwitz
Canes, Helena	23-10-1934	Amsterdam	28-05-1943	Sobibor
Canes, Hendrika	19-09-1928	Amsterdam	09-08-1942	Auschwitz
Canes, Henny	19-10-1925	Amsterdam	28-05-1943	Sobibor
Canes, Henny	10-10-1930	Amsterdam	04-06-1943	Sobibor
Canes, Henri	08-09-1917	Amsterdam	31-03-1944	Auschwitz
Canes, Isaac	16-12-1910	Amsterdam	09-07-1943	Auschwitz
Canes, Israel	02-08-1931	Amsterdam	23-07-1943	Auschwitz
Canes, Jack	10-07-1922	Amsterdam	30-9-1942	Auschwitz
Canes, Jansje	21-06-1876	Amsterdam	13-03-1943	Sobibor
Canes, Jansje	05-11-1891	Amsterdam	12-10-1942	Auschwitz
Canes, Jansje	04-09-1905	Amsterdam	04-06-1943	Sobibor
Canes, Jansje	06-01-1906	Amsterdam	09-04-1943	Sobibor
Canes, Jansje	12-05-1922	Amsterdam	30-09-1942	Auschwitz
Canes, Jansje	10-10-1926	Amsterdam	30-09-1942	Auschwitz
Canes, Jansje	15-06-1928	Amsterdam	14-09-1942	Auschwitz
Canes, Jansje	14-01-1929	Amsterdam	02-04-1943	Sobibor
Canes, Jesaija	15-08-1895	Amsterdam	30-09-1942	Auschwitz

	DATE OF BIRTH	PLACE OF BIRTH	DATE OF DEATH	PLACE OF DEATH
Canes, Joseph	16-01-1867	Amsterdam	13-03-1943	Sobibor
Canes, Joseph	26-05-1882	Amsterdam	13-03-1943	Sobibor
Canes, Joseph	26-03-1896	Amsterdam	28-05-1943	Sobibor
Canes, Joseph	27-06-1899	Amsterdam	04-06-1943	Sobibor
Canes, Jozeph	11-06-1922	Amsterdam	31-01-1943	Auschwitz
Canes, Juda	17-01-1880	Amsterdam	14-09-1942	Auschwitz
Canes, Karel Meijer	06-06-1941	Amsterdam	23-07-1942	Auschwitz
Canes, Lea	12-04-1895	Amsterdam	11-06-1943	Sobibor
Canes, Leman	09-08-1888	Amsterdam	06-09-1944	Auschwitz
Canes, Leman	13-03-1893	Amsterdam	28-02-1943	Auschwitz
Canes, Levie	21-09-1917	Amsterdam	02-03-1944	Utrecht
Canes, Liepman	31-12-1886	Amsterdam	09-07-1943	Sobibor
Canes, Lion	30-04-1917	Amsterdam	30-09-1942	Auschwitz
Canes, Louis	19-10-1894	Amsterdam	31-12-1942	Auschwitz
Canes, Louis	21-10-1898	Amsterdam	14-05-1943	Sobibor
Canes, Marcus	26-03-1932	Amsterdam	20-03-1943	Sobibor
Canes, Matje	28-09-1893	Amsterdam	08-10-1942	Auschwitz
Canes, Maurits	18-05-1902	Amsterdam	30-09-1942	Auschwitz
Canes, Maurits	11-09-1918	Amsterdam	31-03-1944	Central Europe
Canes, Maurits	12-02-1924	Amsterdam	30-09-1942	Auschwitz
Canes, Meijer	02-09-1901	Amsterdam	25-01-1943	Auschwitz
Canes, Meijer	06-05-1924	Amsterdam	28-02-1943	Auschwitz
Canes, Mia	29-07-1935	Amsterdam	23-07-1943	Auschwitz
Canes, Mietje	06-01-1888	Amsterdam	27-08-1943	Auschwitz
Canes, Mietje	11-03-1899	Amsterdam	07-12-1942	Auschwitz
Canes, Mozes	05-02-1868	Amsterdam	20-03-1943	Sobibor
Canes, Mozes	16-01-1890	Amsterdam	04-06-1943	Sobibor
Canes, Mozes	20-12-1897	Amsterdam	28-05-1943	Sobibor
Canes, Mozes	26-02-1914	Amsterdam	03-09-1942	Auschwitz
Canes, Mozes	04-05-1923	Amsterdam	30-09-1942	Auschwitz
Canes, Mozes	15-09-1931	Amsterdam	10-09-1943	Auschwitz
Canes, Naatje	28-04-1892	Amsterdam	28-05-1943	Sobibor
Canes, Nathan	10-03-1897	Amsterdam	30-09-1942	Auschwitz
Canes, Philip	07-08-1879	Amsterdam	03-09-1943	Auschwitz
Canes, Raatje	20-07-1895	Amsterdam	05-10-1942	Auschwitz

	DATE OF BIRTH	PLACE OF BIRTH	DATE OF DEATH	PLACE OF DEATH
Canes, Rachel	09-12-1921	Amsterdam	30-04-1943	Sobibor
Canes, Raphael Sadok	07-10-1868	Amsterdam	16-04-1943	Sobibor
Canes, Rebecca	28-02-1884	Amsterdam	04-06-1943	Sobibor
Canes, Rebecca	30-11-1916	Amsterdam	06-10-1944	Auschwitz
Canes, Rebecca	09-12-1928	Amsterdam	03-09-1943	Auschwitz
Canes, Rosa	10-07-1874	Rotterdam	02-11-1942	Auschwitz
Canes, Rosa	07-01-1914	Amsterdam	31-01-1944	Auschwitz
Canes, Rosette	21-07-1912	Amsterdam	01-05-1944	Birkenau
Canes, Saartje	22-11-1899	Amsterdam	10-09-1942	Auschwitz
Canes, Saartje	04-07-1897	Amsterdam	24-09-1943	Auschwitz
Canes, Salomon	01-10-1861	Amsterdam	21-05-1943	Sobibor
Canes, Salomon	07-11-1891	Amsterdam	30-11-1942	Central Europe
Canes, Salomon	25-07-1894	Amsterdam	30-09-1942	Auschwitz
Canes, Salomon	09-10-1896	Amsterdam	31-03-1944	Central Europe
Canes, Salomon	10-04-1903	Amsterdam	15-02-1944	Warsaw
Canes, Salomon	14-02-1920	Amsterdam	31-03-1944	Central Europe
Canes, Salomon	02-06-1921	Amsterdam	26-01-1944	Auschwitz
Canes, Samson	04-04-1871	Amsterdam	05-03-1943	Sobibor
Canes, Samuel	05-12-1884	Amsterdam	09-07-1943	Sobibor
Canes, Samuel Gaim	17-10-1877	Amsterdam	31-10-1944	Auschwitz
Canes, Sander	14-04-1901	Amsterdam	28-02-1943	Auschwitz
Canes, Sara	08-03-1878	Amsterdam	14-09-1942	Auschwitz
Canes, Sara	12-10-1892	Amsterdam	08-10-1942	Auschwitz
Canes, Sara	13-10-1911	Amsterdam	01-07-1943	Sobibor
Canes, Sara	03-07-1932	Amsterdam	02-04-1943	Sobibor
Canes, Sarah	13-7-1903	Antwerpen	11-06-1943	Sobibor
Canes, Selly	09-02-1932	Amsterdam	04-06-1943	Sobibor
Canes, Seline	01-04-1912	Amsterdam	02-07-1943	Sobibor
Canes, Simon	08-05-1896	Amsterdam	04-06-1943	Sobibor
Canes, Sippora	21-12-1876	Rotterdam	02-11-1942	Auschwitz
Canes, Sophia	05-12-1873	Amsterdam	28-05-1943	Auschwitz
Canes, Tobias	05-07-1896	Amsterdam	11-06-1943	Sobibor
Canes, Vogeltje	09-05-1867	Amsterdam	28-09-1942	Auschwitz
Canes, Vrouwtje	31-08-1872	Amsterdam	28-09-1942	Auschwitz
Kanes, Abraham	04-02-1878	Amsterdam	21-01-1943	Auschwitz

	DATE OF BIRTH	PLACE OF BIRTH	DATE OF DEATH	PLACE OF DEATH
Kanes, Abraham	08-11-1887	Amsterdam	12-02-1943	Auschwitz
Kanes, Abraham	19-12-1905	Amsterdam	11-06-1943	Sobibor
Kanes, Barend	28-04-1872	Amsterdam	15-12-1942	Auschwitz
Kanes, Barend	15-08-1940	Amsterdam	29-07-1942	Auschwitz
Kanes, Barend	20-07-1942	Amsterdam	02-07-1943	Sobibor
Kanes, Esther	25-04-1935	Amsterdam	29-07-1942	Auschwitz
Kanes, Grietje	23-10-1890	Amsterdam	23-11-1942	Auschwitz
Kanes, Hartog	29-07-1917	Amsterdam	31-01-1944	Auschwitz
Kanes, Hijman	16-10-1892	Amsterdam	31-10-1943	Franke
Kanes, Isaac	15-08-1920	Amsterdam	21-01-1945	Blechhammer
Kanes, Israel	29-01-1915	Amsterdam	28-02-1943	Auschwitz
Kanes, Israel	20-10-1919	Amsterdam	02-07-1943	Sobibor
Kanes, Jacob	13-01-1887	Amsterdam	05-11-1942	Auschwitz
Kanes, Jacob	24-11-1891	Amsterdam	28-02-1943	Auschwitz
Kanes, Jacob	16-06-1895	Amsterdam	30-11-1943	Auschwitz
Kanes, Lea	18-04-1935	Amsterdam	11-06-1943	Sobibor
Kanes, Lena	18-02-1917	Amsterdam	31-01-1944	Auschwitz
Kanes, Levie	20-02-1885	Amsterdam	23-04-1943	Sobibor
Kanes, Louis	14-07-1910	Amsterdam	31-03-1944	Auschwitz
Kanes, Louis	21-07-1932	Amsterdam	14-05-1943	Sobibor
Kanes, Maurits	21-09-1911	Amsterdam	30-09-1942	Auschwitz
Kanes, Mina	28-03-1882	Amsterdam	23-11-1942	Auschwitz
Kanes, Philip	11-01-1922	Amsterdam	24-01-1944	Auschwitz
Kanes, Rachel	17-11-1899	Amsterdam	09-04-1943	Sobibor
Kanes, Rebecca Lea	24-08-1943	Westerbork	19-11-1943	Auschwitz
Kanes, Roosje	30-10-1897	Amsterdam	02-04-1943	Sobibor
Kanes, Saartje	13-05-1880	Amsterdam	23-11-1942	Auschwitz
Kanes, Salomon	18-06-1914	Amsterdam	16-01-1944	Auschwitz
Kanes, Samson	08-0801913	Amsterdam	11-06-1943	Sobibor
Kanes, Sara	03-05-1891	Amsterdam	21-05-1943	Sobibor
Kanes, Sara	26-11-1922	Amsterdam	02-07-1943	Sobibor
Kanes, Schoontje	05-03-1876	Amsterdam	05-02-1943	Auschwitz
Kanes, Schoontje	17-11-1893	Amsterdam	23-11-1943	Auschwitz
Kanes, Schoontje	15-05-1896	Amsterdam	21-01-1943	Auschwitz
Kanes, Schoontje	03-05-1914	Amsterdam	04-06-1943	Auschwitz

	DATE OF BIRTH	PLACE OF BIRTH	DATE OF DEATH	PLACE OF DEATH
Kanes, Sebina	21-03-1879	Amsterdam	26-03-1943	Sobibor
Kanes, Simon	03-05-1940	Amsterdam	03-05-1943	Sobibor
Kanes, Vrouwtje	30-10-1889	Amsterdam	26-10-1942	Auschwitz
Kanes-Eisendraht, Adelheid	09-04-1881	Amsterdam	11-10-1944	Auschwitz
Kanes-Hamburg, Esther	25-05-1876	Amsterdam	23-04-1943	Sobibor
Kanes-Hond, Suze	15-06-1919	Amsterdam	02-07-1943	Sobibor
Kanes-Jas, Raatje	30-05-1889	Amsterdam	12-02-1943	Auschwitz
Kanes-Kanter, Betje	24-11-1923	Amsterdam	02-07-1943	Sobibor
Kanes-Korper, Johanna	27-05-1904	Amsterdam	19-11-1943	Auschwitz
Kanes-Lootsteen, Esther	01-01-1901	Amsterdam	02-11-1942	Auschwitz
Kanes-Melkman, Femmina	26-03-1918	Amsterdam	30-04-1945	Karlstad
Kanes-Mug, Schoontje	09-10-1882	Amsterdam	21-01-1943	Auschwitz
Kanes-Prins, Klaartje	14-11-1890	Amsterdam	22-05-1944	Auschwitz
Kanes-de Rood, Betje	29-02-1889	Amsterdam	23-11-1942	Auschwitz
Kanes-Rootveld, Branca	26-09-1918	Amsterdam	31-01-1944	Auschwitz
Kanes-Scheffer, Betje	25-07-1913	Amsterdam	11-06-1943	Sobibor
Kanes-Schellevis, Duifje	13-04-1864	Amsterdam	09-04-1943	Sobibor
Kanes-Visser, Rebecca	05-07-1909	Amsterdam	11-06-1943	Sobibor
Kanes-Vogel, Heintje	11-03-1897	Amsterdam	14-05-1943	Sobibor
Kanes-de Vries, Johanna	06-02-1888	Amsterdam	05-02-1943	Auschwitz
Kanes-Winnik, Rebecca	08-11-1913	Amsterdam	29-07-1942	Auschwitz
Kanes-Zwalf, Lea	10-12-1875	Amsterdam	30-04-1943	Sobibor